First published in the United States of America in 1995 by WRS Publishing, a division of WRS Group, Inc., 701 N. New Road, Waco, Texas 76710
Book design by Kenneth Turbeville
Jacket design by Joe James

10 9 8 7 6 5 4 3 2 1

Library of Congress Catalog Card Number

ISBN-1-56796-055-3

Dedication

To my mother and father,
Dory and Louie,
who have always given me
love and strength.

Acknowledgments

I would like to thank the many people who have encouraged me and helped me through the process of putting together this program. Specifically, those people include my wife, Robbin, who has taught me more about love and relationships than I ever dreamed possible; my parents, Louie and Dory Amen, who have always encouraged me with love and kindness; my children, Antony, Breanne, and Kaitlyn, who are the reason to write about successful relationships to give them a map to make their way easier. In addition, I'd like to thank my staff, Ronnette Leonard, Robert Gessler, Shelley Bernhart, and Donna Greene, for their ideas, encouragement, and support. Also, thanks to Dottie Walters, for her ideas, encouragement, and support. And to Dr. Wayman Spence, who had faith enough in me and the project to bring it to the marketplace.

Table of Contents

Introduction

Would you give two minutes a day for a lifetime of love? Of course you would! Few things, if any, are more important in life than love. Yet most people spend more time planning for the Christmas holidays or for vacations than they do planning their lives with another person. The results of such a lack of focus can be tension, heartache, and loneliness. The life plan detailed in *Would You Give Two Minutes a Day for a Lifetime of Love?* will give couples the basic skills and information they need to have positive, satisfying relationships. The plan is simple. It involves developing a "Two-Minute Focus Statement," and then devoting two minutes a day to reviewing that statement.

If couples are willing to invest the small amount of time needed to make the plan work, the result will be a relationship that maintains a *total focus* and is more fulfilling than they dreamed possible.

Over the past thirty years, intimate relationships have faced innumerable dangers. Marriages continue to break up at record rates, blurred gender roles add to the difficulties, and the fast pace of our society is causing many couples to lose track of each other as they race through their lives. Yet, intimate relationships do not have to fall victim to these modern challenges.

Would You Give Two Minutes a Day for a Lifetime of Love? is a program designed to help couples develop a clear, written focus for their relationships that incorporates communication, sexuality, work, money, fun, and child-rearing. By following specific steps, couples will learn to understand the reasons behind their behavior in a relationship and to develop the motivation for positive change. The program will also teach partners to develop the skills that will result in a productive and fulfilling relationship.

A bank rarely lends money to a new business that

cannot produce a business plan. Such a plan offers evidence that the owners have thought out the business's purpose, its goals, and have developed a strategy to reach those goals. Without a solid business plan, a company is likely to fail. Yet, people who begin personal relationships (which can be much more complicated than business) seldom develop a clear plan together. It is unbelievable that we spend more time teaching our children to diagram sentences or memorize ancient historical facts than how to handle their day-to-day relationships effectively. No wonder relationships are failing at such a high rate.

Most of us lack some skill in relating to others. Too often, couples drift apart because of job pressures, emotional problems, or misunderstandings. Through my work as a psychiatrist, I have come to the conclusion that problems between people do not occur because couples lack desire for good relationships; rather, the problems involve a lack of focus and a need for better skills. When I teach couples the appropriate relationship skills and how to obtain total focus, the relationship improves rapidly and permanently.

I developed *Would You Give Two Minutes a Day for a Lifetime of Love?* out of twelve years of day-to-day clinical work with couples. This program is meant for couples to work together. Although individuals in a relationship can gain significant benefit from working the program alone, it is most effective when both partners are committed to its success. The program works best when both partners read a chapter at a time, work through the exercises, and discuss what they learn.

One of the first steps is to examine other people's relationships that you admire and those that you don't. Couples will learn the principles of effective negotiation and will work together to establish a Two-Minute Focus Statement. The next step is to explore goals involving such elements as communication, time together, raising kids, and sexuality. Next, couples will study how work and financial situations affect their lives together and they will learn to establish joint goals. Readers will explore how the relationship can support the personal goals of each partner, including physical, emotional, and spiritual health. Then you'll be shown how to put these goals into your Two-Minute Focus Statement, which you'll review every day to keep your thoughts and behavior on track. The program also presents effective monitoring and revision techniques to help to cover any potential changes. Interactive worksheets and questionnaires will be used to help you understand your motivation and establish your focus.

Those who follow this plan will have engaged their partners in meaningful discussions about their lives together. The resulting Two-Minute Focus Statement will guide couples toward more positive thoughts, attitudes, and actions.

Chapter 1

Two-Minute Focus:
The concept

Your Two-Minute Focus Statement can be put together in a week, but its impact may last a lifetime.

The most common problem in troubled relationships is a lack of focus. People in such relationships have few cohesive principles to drive them in a healthy direction. They seem stuck in ineffective behavior patterns, and thus become more vulnerable to everyday problems and stresses.

Clinically, when couples are able to focus on what really matters in their lives together, they begin to behave more effectively in the relationship. Several years ago, I developed a computer worksheet for couples simply titled "Goals." On this worksheet, I asked them to write out their specific desires for each aspect of their relationship (time together, communication, sex, parenting, work). Then we completed and refined the worksheet together in my office. The couple's assignment was then to post it where both parties could review it every day. It took them about two minutes a day to review.

Many couples noticed astonishing results. Negativity in the relationships decreased and positive and supportive behavior increased. I changed the title from "Goals" to "One-Page Miracle" because of the astonishing results. Getting people focused on what they want in their relationship has a dramatic effect on their behavior. The key to improvement is inducing a couple to be "conscious" of their desires for their relationship, and then to encourage them to match their behavior to what they want!

BIOCHEMICAL GHOSTS FROM THE PAST

If partners do not clearly focus their thoughts and behavior on what they want, they will tend to slip into unconscious thoughts, feelings, and behavior patterns from the past that are stored in their brains. A certain part of the brain, the basal ganglia, stores patterns of learned behavior. The basal ganglia store information about how to be a father, how to be a mother, how to be a husband or a wife, a son or a daughter—even a parent or grandparent. As we go through life, our brain stores and categorizes much of what we experience, especially emotionally charged experiences. Each interaction, observation, or experience is chemically housed in the brain cells that are associated with that type of event. Imagine relationship or marriage "houses" in the center of your brain. The information stored in these houses comes from many sources: from the interaction we saw between our parents, our grandparents, our friends' parents, television role models, etc.

Once these patterns, thoughts, and feelings are stored, a significant association can trigger them at a moment's notice. Usually we are unconscious of or unaware of what is happening. Our memory works through association, where one event sparks memories of similar events from the past. For example, if we saw our parents repeatedly handle conflict by yelling, screaming, or even hitting each other, that pattern of behavior, or fighting, which is stored in the "marriage house" in the brain may be unconsciously turned on when, as adults, a fight or a disagreement occurs.

Becoming conscious of our goals and desires is the best way to overcome these unconscious, stored patterns from the past. If we never clearly focus our behavior, we are doomed to play out the messages stored in our brains.

The following is a case example to illustrate how stored messages affect behavior. When Jack was growing up, he had two radically different models for marriage.

His parents' relationship was dominated by a father who was considered king. Jack's father was off at work most of the time while his mother ran the day-to-day household affairs. Yet, when his father came home, he was the boss. No one questioned that fact, especially not his mother (at least not in Jack's presence). Watching his parents' relationship year after year stored an expectation in his "marriage house" in the basal ganglia of his brain that men are in charge at home and their word is law, even though they are not there much. Jack never liked that system much, and as a teenager he told himself that he would allow his wife to be more of a part of the decision-making process. His conscious thought was working against unconscious stored behavior patterns.

Jack's maternal grandparents, however, presented a different marital style from his parents'. When he was growing up, Jack was close to his grandfather. His grandfather seemed the opposite of his father. He was at home more, helpful, and dominated by Jack's grandmother, who at times, didn't seem to treat her husband that nicely. Her word seemed to carry more weight, and Jack's grandfather did whatever he could to please her. Jack remembered being irritated by his grandfather's conciliatory attitude toward his grandmother.

You can imagine how confusing this all was for Jack when he got married. Consciously, he wanted to have a kind, caring, loving, and supportive relationship with his wife. Yet, stored in his brain were messages like:

- "She should listen to me and my word should be the law."
- "The wife handles the day-to-day workings of the home while I work."
- "I don't want my wife to dominate me the way my grandmother dominated my grandfather."

Jack's wife, Carlita, on the other hand, came into the relationship with her own stored messages. Carlita came from a family with a negative mother and an alcoholic father. Year after year, her parents fought. She witnessed anger, hostility, turmoil, and physical abuse. She received many negative messages about marriage. In addition, Carlita had been married once before to a man who turned out to be both an alcoholic and physically abusive toward her. Now, her goal in her marriage to Jack was the same as his: to have a kind, caring, loving, and supportive relationship. But the unconscious messages stored in her basal ganglia about marriage were negative. Some of these negative messages included:

- "Protect yourself or you will be hurt."
- "You can't trust the person to whom you are married."
- "Be on guard."
- "Be able to leave at a moment's notice."

No wonder Jack and Carlita had problems. Even after seeing four marriage counselors, their stored unconscious messages were obstructing their goal of having a great marriage. By the time they came to see me, they had just split up for the second time and were desperate for help. They both said they wanted the marriage to work, but just couldn't seem to live together without fighting. They usually fought over little things. Neither was having an affair, being dishonest, drinking too much, or using drugs. They were both nice people stuck in the patterns of their past.

Uncovering these messages was essential for their healing. Even more important, however, was keeping them totally focused on their goals with the Two-Minute Focus Statement. The statement helped them to develop new associations to keep their behavior effective "in the moment." Conscious desires and unconscious motivation can be at odds with each other if you are not focused.

ANTIDOTE FOR THE BIOCHEMICAL GHOSTS AND THE RAT RACE

The Two-Minute Focus Statement is an antidote for unconscious behavior. By clearly focusing your thoughts and behavior, you dramatically increase your chances of getting what you want. Your actions become consistent with your goals, your words become more effective, and the motivation for your behavior becomes clear. Clear focus is not only important in intimate relationships. It is helpful in parenting (to avoid repeating the mistakes your parents made with you), business (no bank would lend you money for a business without a clear business plan), health, and personal finance. Unfortunately, as I said in the introduction, most people spend more time planning for Christmas or their summer vacations than they do planning and focusing their lives. You will be different.

Without clear focus, relationships also can be battered by the forces and pressures of the day (the rat race). In many ways, modern living is not conducive to fostering healthy relationships. Two-parent, working families are almost always stretched for time, commuting families are tired by the end of the day, high mortgage payments add additional pressures, economic uncertainties cause individual and family anxiety, and television continually scares us (the evening news) and shows us how life "ought to be" through its programming. Blurred gender roles and a lessening of the church's influence on individual lives also add to the confusion. No wonder relationships are in trouble. The Two-Minute Focus Statement overcomes such daily pressures by giving couples a road map that leads to where they want to be together.

OVERCOMING BURNOUT AND MID-LIFE CRISES

Balance is a special feature of the Two-Minute Focus Statement. In this program we'll look at the interactive qualities of your relationship, how children, work, and finances impact the relationship, as well as the influence of individual wants and needs (physical, emotional, and spiritual). Focusing your relationship entails gaining a balance between the needs of the individual and the relationship, children, work, and finances, enabling a couple to better prevent burnout and the bumps that happen to many people along the way. I have treated many men and women who have gone through mid-life crises in their relationships. I am convinced that these painful times were due mostly to a lack of knowledge, a lack of planning, a lack of balance, and a lack of focus.

Here is a typical mid-life scenario: A man and woman get married in their early twenties. Initially, both work, or they are in college. The couple then decides to have a family. The woman focuses significant energy at home caring for her family, while the man focuses most of his energy at work, trying to adequately provide for his family. After eight to twelve years of this, both the husband and wife are worn out. They do not have enough time together, they're tired, and they are spending inordinate amounts of time on work or family activities and little time on their relationship. They begin to miss intimacy, but find little in each other. They may begin to look for intimacy from other people. Also, at this point, the man may be established enough in his career to want to spend more time at home. But the woman, who is not accustomed to having him home, may begin to long for a career. They end up missing each other as they pass through their lives, leaving them vulnerable to a crisis.

The Two-Minute Focus Statement will help couples maintain proper focus and balance to prevent burnout and the life crises to which we are all vulnerable.

UNLOCKING YOUR MIND'S POWER

Getting a clear picture in your mind is essential to making anything happen. Your brain can only make happen what it can see and imagine. Focusing on what you want will help you get what you want. Focusing on the negative will only invite disaster. Your brain is powerful.

One of the best human examples of this phenomenon is a medical condition called "pseudocyesis," which means false pregnancy. This occurs when a woman believes she is pregnant so strongly that her body takes on the shape and function of pregnancy, even though not pregnant. I treated a forty-two-year-old woman who wanted to be pregnant so badly that she was consumed with thoughts of pregnancy. Finally, she thought it happened. She stopped having periods, her breasts were enlarged and even excreted small amounts of liquid, her belly began to swell, and she even had some unusual cravings. Yet, when she went to the doctor, her pregnancy test was negative. Again and again. When the ultrasound revealed no evidence of a pregnancy, the obstetrician sent this woman to see me.

Beliefs are powerful. Consciously use your imagination to direct your thoughts and behavior toward your lover.

Chapter 2

Mentors, Friends, Intruders, and Others:

Looking at the people who help your relationships and those who don't

Ann and Wayne had been married forty-seven years when my wife and I lived across the street from them. We spent a lot of time with them, going to ball games, talking on the sidewalk, sharing meals. It was obvious that they loved each other as much then as when they were first married. They were attentive, affectionate, kind, and polite to each other. They talked openly about their relationship, but always with respect for each other. Being with them encouraged my wife and me to treat each other more as they did. The secrets to their success, Wayne told me, were mutual respect, fun, and not taking the little things too seriously. He said, "There are a thousand things we can fight about, but who wants to? We would rather spend our time loving and playing with each other. Too many couples get caught up fighting about nothing. We don't have time for that."

Dottie and Bob Walters had been married forty-nine years when Dottie came into our lives. She is a world-renowned expert on the speaking business and the author of *Speak and Grow Rich* and *The Greatest Speakers I Ever Heard*, and I had sought her help in developing my speaking career. One evening my wife and I had the privilege of taking Dottie to an author's party in San Francisco. We picked her up at the hotel near the airport and started the twenty-mile trip to downtown San Francisco. As fate would have it, we hit a traffic jam. The thirty-minute trip took an hour and a half, and I was glad it did. Dottie told us some of the secrets of her marriage to Bob. "My father left me when I was young," she said. "When I first met Bob and saw how truly kind he was, I knew I'd marry him. It's not always been easy, but I've learned to let go of the small things and focus on the good things. That's helped the most." She continued, "When we were first married I wanted Bob to do the yard work. He didn't want to. He didn't like yard work and would rather spend his time doing other things. I carried some resentment over it until I realized what a small thing it was. After all, I could work (she sold newspaper advertising space), sell an extra ad, and hire a gardener to do the yard. What a small price to pay for a good man. He was certainly worth that to me." She also told us about a study she read where one of the greatest irritations women have is that their men do not put down the toilet seat. "How silly," she said. "Why make a big deal out of putting down the toilet seat? Having Bob means more to me than what I have to do in the bathroom." Dottie told us that the secret of a long and happy marriage is being able to recognize more of the good things than the bad in a relationship. "You get what you think about," Dottie said.

Rod and Cathy were the opposite of Ann and Wayne and Dottie and Bob. They fought constantly over little things, belittled each other at social gatherings, and expressed their disappointment in each other to any friends who would listen. Cathy felt that Rod wasn't financially successful enough to take proper care of their family. Cathy had grown up in an upper middle-class family, and she was used to being able to spend as much money as she wanted. Rod was much more interested in his hobbies and in spending time with the children than in working himself to death. Rod complained that Cathy was spoiled, cold, and critical.

He felt that sex depended on whether he doted on Cathy. He called her "the war department" because of their frequent fights. I noticed that people who were around them tended to complain about their own spouses as well. The negativity had a certain contagious quality.

MENTORS

In developing total focus for your relationship, it is helpful to study those relationships you admire and those you don't. By doing this, you establish definitive guidelines for your own behavior. Ask yourself:
Who are the couples you admire?
- What are their qualities?
- How do they talk to each other?
- How do they touch each other?
- How do they talk about each other?

Who are the couples you don't admire?
- What are their qualities?
- How do they talk to each other?
- How do they touch each other?
- How do they talk about each other?

Here are two special "mentor" couples from my own life that have had a powerful influence on my wife and me.

George, an outstanding professor of family practice medicine at my medical school, and his wife, Betty, were close. They taught us by word and example how successful couples live. They spent hours talking with each other. They held hands, gave each other loving looks, and talked about each other in special ways. They were involved in giving to other people together. They taught a family life course for medical students, and they took a personal interest in many of the students and their families. Once, when Betty became sick and spent a couple of days in the hospital where most of the medical students worked, I saw how they reacted under pressure. I saw the love in George's eyes when he held Betty's hand. This was no show for others. Their bond was truly special.

Several years ago my wife and I spent some time in Boston, visiting Stan and Carol. Stan was the chairman of the psychiatry department where I went to medical school. He was the single most influential person in my decision to become a psychiatrist. When I went to medical school, I had planned to be a pediatrician, but after I took courses with Stan and watched him work with patients, I wanted to do what he did. He had real people skills and was able to help people who had deep emotional hurts, "soul pain." Stan's wife, Carol, spent a lot of time encouraging the medical students and their spouses. She taught the spouses what it is like being married to a doctor, and she taught all of us strategies to maintain a helpful, healing marriage in the midst of busy careers. Together, Stan and Carol complimented each other. Their relationship was based on togetherness, support, and love. They traveled together, taught Sunday School at church together, raised their children in a positive way together, and treated each other with respect. They shared with us that their relationship was not always perfect. Early on, Stan worked a lot and he needed to be alone after listening to people with problems all day long. It took Carol some time to get used to this, but they were able to work it out by using their faith in God and their time together. Working together was important to them.

When we saw Stan and Carol in Boston, we realized what a powerful impact they had had on our lives. Stan was my mentor, and together, Stan and Carol were mentors for my wife and me. They helped me to realize how important it is to have mentors, people to look up to. Individually and as a couple, mentors are very important.

Unfortunately, many couples never develop solid mentor relationships. Either they do not look for the opportunity, or their attitude of "knowing it all" or being unteachable hinders them. Those who never establish this type of a relationship lose a lot, since successful couples have so much to teach us.

In the same vein, do other couples look up to your relationship? Take an inventory of who you think looks up to you. Whose life are you helping to shape? How do you treat that person? Are you helping to uplift that person or are you barely paying attention? These are critical questions for a mentor.

If you recognize who your mentors are, do you take a few minutes to tell them how important they have been in your life? Call them, write them, or find some way to let them know they have touched your life in a special way.

QUALITIES YOU ADMIRE AND THOSE YOU DON'T

Here is a list of the qualities that I've seen in couples I admire and those that I don't. Compare them to your experience.

Admirable qualities:
- kindness
- good listeners
- respect
- loving playfulness
- verbal and nonverbal displays of affection
- reliability
- trust
- loyalty
- genuine commitment
- polite and mannerly
- thoughtful

Undesirable qualities:
- jump to conclusions
- predict the worst
- cruelty
- negativity
- aloofness
- degrade each other
- rudeness

- complaining
- heavy use of alcohol or drugs
- sense of superiority
- lack of commitment
- selfishness
- anger
- hostility
- flirtatiousness
- one-upmanship games
- thoughtlessness

Remember, things are not always as they seem. No one I know has a perfect relationship. Take the qualities you admire in others and focus on them for your relationship. Notice the qualities you dislike and work on avoiding them.

Ann and Wayne, Dottie and Bob, George and Betty, and Stan and Carol have shared much happiness together. Cathy and Rod have shared tension, anger, disappointment, and frustration. Understanding the difference will help you mold your relationship so that you receive more of what you want.

YOUR FRIENDS MATTER

Friendships can have a positive influence on a relationship, or they can have a divisive or negative impact. Roberta and Jim were newlyweds. Jim was fresh out of the Marines. Like most newly married couples, they were struggling to establish a sense of unity. They had both come from dysfunctional families and were having a more difficult time than most couples. Then Larry showed up. Larry was a Marine buddy of Jim's. In fact, they were often drinking and carousing buddies. After Larry was dishonorably discharged from the Marines after his third DUI (driving under the influence), he had trouble finding work. He had kept in contact with Jim who, at the time, was working for a plumbing contractor. The contractor needed extra help, and Jim told Larry to come to their town.

Initially, Roberta liked Larry. He was funny and

polite. She had reservations when Jim asked her if Larry could live with them, but Jim assured her it would only be for a short period of time. At first things went well. Larry helped around the house and Jim seemed happy to have the company of an old friend. But then the nightmare began. Jim and Larry started to get drunk together. They tried to make Roberta feel guilty whenever she complained about their drinking. "After all," they said, "we worked hard all day. Aren't we entitled to some fun?" Jim and Larry also started to stay out late. They would laugh together about how Larry was "scoring" with women. Roberta became even more worried. She wondered what Jim was doing while Larry "scored." She didn't have to wonder for long. She found Jim and Larry drunk, in their van in the garage with two other women. Roberta gave Jim an ultimatum (perhaps later than was helpful) and Larry moved out. Their relationship had been damaged irreparably, however, and it ended several months later. Friends can have a negative impact on relationships.

Friends also can have a positive impact. Alan and Amy had just gotten married when they met Don and Laurie who lived downstairs from them. They had three children, were devout Christians, and treated each other with love and respect. Alan and Amy spent a lot of time in Don and Laurie's home. They played games together, went to church together, and shared many meals. As newlyweds, Alan and Amy had a lot to learn about the day-to-day business of being married. Don and Laurie were good teachers.

What friends do you have as a couple? (List their names.)

Do they help you as a couple, or do they hurt you?

Who are your individual friends? (List their names.)

Do they enhance your relationship with your partner or do they detract from it?

Mentors, friends, and others play a significant role in your relationships. Make sure they fit into the goals you have for your life as a couple.

Chapter 3

Establishing the Principles and Culture of Your Relationship:

Are your hearts and minds together?

Principle:
A code of conduct

Culture:
The integrated pattern of human behavior that includes thought, speech, action, and artifacts and depends upon man's capacity for learning and transmitting knowledge to succeeding generations.
—*Merriam-Webster's New Collegiate Dictionary*

To develop total focus, couples must clearly define a set of principles or a "culture" on which to base their behavior. Otherwise, they might end up like Bill and Sarah. To the outside world, Bill and Sarah seemed a good match. They went to church together, participated in school functions for their children, and worked together in the family business. In private, however, they were often cruel to each other. They fought over little things and they were turning nastier as the years passed. Frequently, they commented critically on each other's parents, used foul language, and called each other names. Negative bantering between them became the rule when they were out of the public eye.

Bill and Sarah sought therapy for themselves after their minister preached a sermon on how children often reflect their parents' attitudes. Their teenage son, Matt, and eleven-year-old-daughter, Lisa, treated each other so negatively that Bill and Sarah could not ignore the problem. Matt continually teased and badgered Lisa, who looked for ways to irritate Matt. No one was having fun at home, and Bill and Sarah did not want their children to end up as unhappy as they were. During therapy sessions it was obvious that the mocking style of interaction between the couple had become a habit. It seemed that every other word out of their mouths toward each other involved a put-down, a needle, or a wisecrack. Once they got going it was hard to stop. During one session, I kept score of the number of negative comments they uttered. Eighty-two in a forty-five-minute session (almost two a minute)!

Early in the therapy, I spoke with Bill and Sarah about marital principles and family culture. They needed a code of conduct (set of principles) to guide their misdirected behavior. They also needed to agree on the kind of culture or atmosphere in which they wanted to live and raise their children. Without clearly defining the culture they wanted, they were doomed to continue in the destructive patterns of the past.

Few couples ever consciously establish a code of conduct for their behavior in a relationship. Agreeing on the guiding principles is the first step to obtain significant behavior changes. The following ten principles will help you establish a culture in which your relationships will thrive.

1. **Honesty/Trust**—Successful relationships are based on honesty and trust. When a person knows that his or her partner is honest, a sense of trust develops that strengthens the relationship. Mistrust and doubt, on the other hand, undermine the basic foundation of the bond. Establishing the principle of trust early in a relationship will pay many dividends in the future. Authentic bonding is the

glue that holds relationships together through the tough times.

I have treated many individuals in therapy, however, who have lied to, cheated, and deceived their partners. Their dishonesty led not only to feelings of guilt and shame; it also caused the person to look for negative traits in the other person as a way to justify their own dishonest behavior. Linda and Hank played out this scenario for years. Linda had been involved in an on-again, off-again affair for twelve years. Whenever Hank was overbearing, Linda put up with it silently and then called her lover. She justified her behavior by magnifying Hank's negative actions. In therapy she discovered that whenever she wanted to see her lover she would set Hank off to justify her upcoming liaison. As long as she continued to have this outlet, I told her, her marriage held no hope. But the situation had lasted too long. Hank finally found out about the affair, and he and Linda ended their marriage.

Without honesty and trust, a relationship is nothing more than a facade, and intimacy is rare. The relationship becomes vulnerable to wandering loyalties. Seek to be honest and develop trust within your relationship. Strive toward integrity. Be who you say you are. Make this a top priority. Whenever your actions might compromise honesty or trust, rethink them to see if they are really worth the potential damage they might do to the relationship.

2. Kindness—This characteristic is often overlooked by those who write about relationships. Yet, it is one of the most important principles for motivating couples to make a relationship work. Hostility (the opposite of kindness) erodes closeness. Being demanding or condescending, displaying chronic anger or irritability, and being thoughtless and selfish cause distance and resentment. In difficult relationships, kindness is often one of the first things to disappear and one of the last things to return in healing.

Kindness nurtures warmth and closeness. Kindness involves thinking about the little things in life that add sparks of care and concern. Kindness in a relationship includes such things as:

- Watching your tone of voice and body posture. Voice tone and body posture can cause an immediate positive or negative reaction. (Watch the comments under your breath.)
- Giving your partner time to unwind after a busy day without bombarding him or her with demands, chores, or problems
- Fixing your partner a cup of coffee or tea when you know he or she might want one
- Letting your partner sleep in when you know he or she is tired after a particularly taxing week
- Leaving little notes to be found when you are apart
- Giving a special touch, look, or word
- Taking the children out for the evening so that your partner can have time by him or herself or with friends
- Planning a special trip alone with your partner
- Asking if he or she needs anything from the store when you go
- Making lunch for him or her to take to work
- Making it easier for the other person to wake up in the morning (a hug, back rub, cup of coffee)
- Simply being with your partner when he or she is feeling down

Look for ways to be kind and helpful to each other. It will enhance the quality of the relationship, establish kindness as part of the culture of the family, and make your relationship a place to spend time healing.

3. Fidelity—Emotional as well as sexual fidelity is a key to making a relationship last. Fidelity means to be faithful in thoughts, words, and actions. Fidelity is commitment to the relationship even when your partner is not in the same room. Fidelity means that it is clear to the world that your mind and heart are committed to the relationship.

There are many ways to show infidelity or to be

unfaithful in a relationship. Having a sexual affair is obvious, but it is usually the subtle infidelities that lead to the bigger problems. These include such things as putting your partner down in front of others, acting in ways you know will embarrass your partner, or allowing your eyes to wander in public. How you treat your partner in the presence of others shows how much you respect him or her, as well as how much you respect yourself. Making jokes at his or her expense or sharing intimate details without permission erodes trust, demonstrates to your partner that you don't think much of him or her, and plants the seeds for anger and retaliation. Be faithful to your partner when you are with others.

Equally dangerous to the relationship is talking to friends and coworkers about your partner's undesirable qualities. Talking negatively about your partner in front of your friends or colleagues undermines your partner's stature in the eyes of others (which will also diminish your stature since you picked the person). It also causes you to think more negatively about your partner to justify your verbal betrayal of them. I once had an accountant who frequently complained about his wife. He referred to her as "the wife" as if she weren't his wife, and made other disparaging remarks about her. His comments made me uncomfortable, and I wondered how their relationship was affected by his attitude. Watch your tongue in front of others, and ask yourself if bad-mouthing your partner to others fits any of the goals you have for the relationship. (As an aside, if you spend much time with people who put down their partners, you are likely to do the same thing. Negativity is contagious. Watch the people with whom you spend time.)

4. Hope—Expect the best. Hopes, dreams, and expectations play a powerful role in what you get out of life. When you expect and hope for the best, your subconscious mind often helps it happen. If you look for hurt and pain, your mind will help you find that as well. What you expect is often what you get.

Ellen's father emotionally and physically abused her as a child. She ran away from home at the age of seventeen, believing that she left her father behind. Unfortunately, he followed her in her unconscious mind. Her ability to trust a man was low. She thought that all men, at some level, were like her father and would abuse her. Whenever a strong relationship with a man began to develop, she did something to undermine it. She forgot dates, acted insanely jealous, or was rude to the friends of the men she dated. When they got upset with her, she accused them of being abusive or hostile. After they stopped coming around, she would tell her friends, "See, I told you men were no good. They can't be trusted."

Our expectations are based on the myriad of experiences we bring from the past, and, even though they are often based on distorted material, these expectations have a profound influence on the way we function in our lives. As in Ellen's case, negative expectations are programmed into our minds at some point along the developmental trail. Statements made by influential people in a child's life (parents, teachers, etc.) have a hypnotic quality. They become firmly embedded in the unconscious and drive the individual in a certain direction. If you are always told you can't, where do you learn you can? Other common negative programming statements that hurt relationships are:

- "Don't get married. It won't work."
- "Men (or women) are only after one thing."
- "If you're not perfect, you're no good."
- "You're stupid. Why can't you do anything right?"
- "You are a disappointment."
- "You can't trust him or her."

These statements don't even have to be uttered directly; they can be conveyed by tone of voice, facial expressions, or behavior. Either way, the child gets the message. If the programming is strong enough, a child who receives messages such as these gets caught in a negative mental state that is hard to break. The unconscious mind, like one in a hypnotic trance, takes the negative programming as fact. Children are unable to objectify the input, so it becomes a part of their belief system.

The expectation of success in a relationship is a powerful force all by itself. In my therapy with couples, I discuss the concept of "Positive Basic Assumptions (PBAs)." PBAs are attitudes of hope and positive expectations. They mean that before you react to your partner's words, deeds, or actions, you assume that he or she cares about you. Every word, thought, and action is processed through the filter of caring or PBAs.

When people assume the worst, these assumptions alone can actually make the situation worse. For example, if a husband comes home late from the office, his wife can choose how she reacts to his lateness. She can assume the worst (Negative Basic Assumption), be angry and accusatory, and say something such as, "You don't care about me; you love your job more than me." Or she can assume the best (PBA), tell him that she appreciates him working so hard for the family, and give him a back rub after a long day. Same situation, different assumptions, dramatically different responses. Which response do you think will make the husband want to come home earlier?

As you believe, so shall you act. Use PBAs to make the best environment for a relationship.

5. Priority—In our busy world, people often get disconnected from the people who are most important to them. Early in their marriage, Betty and Warren swore it would never happen to them. Betty worked as a nurse at a local hospital, and Warren was in graduate school studying to be an accountant. They spent hours together, on picnics, going to movies, taking walks along the seashore. Then the children came. Their time alone together was cut in half. Warren graduated from school and joined a large accounting firm. To make a good impression on the senior accountants, he put in long hours at the office. Their time was cut further.

They joined a country club where they would be with the "right kind of people." Their lovemaking dropped from about three times a week to less than twice a month. Resentment and distance crept into their relationship. To make their life together what they thought it should be, they allowed themselves to become too busy. As they watched their best friends file for divorce, they made a conscious decision to rediscover their lost priorities and reset their course before it was too late. They began saying no to activities that did not fit into their goal of having a loving relationship and family.

Like Betty and Warren, the life my wife and I lead can be pretty hectic if we lose our focus. One Saturday when I was driving home, I saw a sign that advertised a dozen roses for $10. It had been a while since I had brought roses home for my wife, so I decided to stop. As I was waiting for the flowers, I thought about how fast my life seemed to be going. I was nearly forty, raising a family, working hard, seeing patients, writing a new book, and paying bills. I barely had enough time to organize my office, let alone my life. Shouldn't I make a simple gesture like bringing home flowers more often? What about priorities? What is more important than my wife? Nothing. Then why did we seem to get only the leftover time together; after the kids, work, chores? Don't you think it is odd that many couples leave their special time to right before bedtime when they are both dead tired? As my mind wandered at the florist's, I decided to buy roses for both of my girls. I knew the look on their faces would bring me great joy. Children are generally easy to please. Just letting them know that you are thinking of them can brighten their whole day. *USA Today* reported a study which said that, on average, parents spend less than seven minutes a week talking alone with their children. How are you doing with your kids?

As I was paying for the flowers, my inner voice began talking to me. *Hey Daniel, who's the one orchestrating your life? The fast pace? Too many demands?*

Did it just happen? Or do you make daily decisions that keep it running in high gear? My mind tried not to hear what came next...

Daniel, remember last night? You challenged a mother in your parenting class who said that she did not have any extra time to spend alone with her daughter who was having emotional problems. The little voice got louder. *You told her that she needed to allocate her time to the important things in her life first, such as her daughter, and perhaps she needed to cut out doing other things that were not as essential. You told her that she is the one who decides how to spend her time. No one can take it from her unless she gives her consent.* I felt a little scolded, but also empowered. If I created the pace of my life, then I could slow it down.

When I walked in the door with the flowers, my girls giggled with excitement. They were so happy their daddy had thought about them—just because, without a special reason. My wife smiled and gave me a big hug. She, too, likes to be thought about, just because. I wondered why I didn't do this more often. Certainly, hugs from my three girls help me feel happy and more connected to life.

How do you spend your time? When is the last time you brought home flowers? When is the last time you held your children and told them they were special, just because? Are you the one who controls the pace of your life? Or is your life controlling you? If you think about it, you get to choose. Prioritize your time to fit your life goals. If your spouse and children are the most important people in your life, make sure you give them the time that is consistent with their place in your heart. Nothing is sadder than a life where the priorities and actions are reversed.

6. Friendship—"Friendship first" is advice I give to all people seeking new relationships. Friendship is the quality that protects a relationship from harm and encourages fun, togetherness, talking, and kinship. *Webster's Dictionary* defines friend as "a person whom one knows, likes, and trusts." Too often I hear about relationships that are based on physical attributes, sexual appeal, and social status, rather than common interests and friendship.

I once treated in psychotherapy a forty-four-year-old, Baptist, corporate executive who was lonely, depressed, and contemplating suicide. Although Stan was successful in business, he had never married. He desired a lasting relationship and he wanted children. He felt that his time was running out. Most of his prior relationships lasted only a few months. He said that he had trouble finding someone who shared his values. Stan was deeply religious and gave much of his time to his church. Out of panic, he began a relationship with a model, Shawn, whom he had met at a party. On a whim, he called Shawn and asked her for a date. To his surprise she accepted and met him for dinner several nights later. Shawn was gorgeous—petite, shapely, and dressed to kill. Her beauty mesmerized Stan. Apparently, Shawn accepted Stan's offer because she had just ended a relationship, and, like Stan, she did not want to be alone. Because of his hopes, Stan ignored the warning signals. Although only twenty-seven, Shawn had had many live-in relationships, and she had subtly suggested that she and Stan use pot together. She backed off when she discovered Stan's religious convictions. Initially, they spent a lot of time together at dinners, on picnics, at the theater, and shopping. They both saw only what they wanted to see, a reflection of what they were seeking, rather than what was really there. After several weeks of dating, they became sexually involved, which was against Stan's beliefs. He rationalized the behavior by talking about marriage with Shawn. Shortly thereafter, they moved in together. Initially, it was bliss. Shawn agreed to go to church with Stan, they talked for hours on the couch, and Shawn was a wonderful cook. Then reality hit. Two of Shawn's old boyfriends began to show up at Stan's home. They looked and dressed scuzzy. They looked like people involved with drugs, and their behavior was hostile and erratic. Shawn just laughed off their visits, though at one point, Stan felt that Shawn was flirting with one of her old flames. Then Shawn's behavior turned erratic. One day she was happy, laughing, and restless, the next she was depressed and mean. When Stan discovered cocaine in the bathroom, he knew the relationship was over. Breaking up with Shawn dashed his hopes, nearly to the point where he wanted to die.

Stan's mistake was allowing his passion and dreams to intrude on reality. He didn't allow time to develop a friendship, to get to know what kind of person Shawn really was. People can appear to be anything for a period of months if it suits their purposes. Shawn was lonely and wanted to be with Stan, so she behaved the way she thought Stan would find attractive. But her behavior was false, as Stan quickly (and painfully) discovered. Become friends first, no matter what age you are starting a relationship.

How do you keep friendship alive in the midst of intimacy? How do you make it a part of the culture of your relationship? Some good questions to ask yourself include:

- "How do I treat my close friends?"
- "Do I treat my partner better than my other close friends?"
- "Do I make time for my partner more a priority than for others?"
- "Am I interested in hearing what my partner has to say?"
- "When something good happens, am I excited to share it with my partner?"
- "When something bad happens, do I long to tell my partner to obtain advice or solace?"

Remember, become friends before lovers. Friendship endures longer than passion.

7. Clear Communication and Assertiveness—Clear communication and assertiveness are important keys to successful relationships. In my experience, one of the underlying problems in many relationships stem from a lack of clear communication and a lack of clearly asserting needs and thoughts. In many cases, when these problems are resolved, other problems also quickly disappear.

For example, Billie Jo was on the verge of divorcing her husband. She felt that she could never please him, and he often seemed gruff and irritated. Although Billie Jo said nothing to her husband, she secretly began to hate him. She developed frequent headaches and neck tension and seemed preoccupied with looking at other men. A friend pushed her to confess her frustrations to her husband. The friend said, "If you're going to leave him anyway, you have little to lose." To Billie Jo's surprise, her husband was shocked by her comments and cried at the possibility of the relationship ending. Billie Jo's husband told her that he was gruff and irritable because his boss was riding him hard at work. He immediately wanted to fix the problems and made Billie Jo promise to talk with him in the future about her feelings. Too often, as mentioned above, people assume the worst about another person and then believe those negative assumptions as fact.

Most people are too wrapped up in themselves to think about what is going on with other people. In relationships, it is critical to be able to state what you need in a clear, positive way. In most situations, the best approach is to be direct. But how you ask is important:

- You can demand (and get hostility);
- You can ask meekly so that no one takes you seriously; or
- You can be firm yet kind in the way you ask and thus get what you need.

How you approach someone greatly affects your success rate in communications.

Listening is essential to good communication. Before you respond to what people say, repeat back what you think they have said to ensure that you have correctly heard them. Statements such as "I hear you saying..."

or "You mean to say..." are the gold standard of good communication. This allows you to confirm what you hear before you respond. It is important to monitor and follow up on your communication. Often it takes repeated efforts to get what you need. It's important not to give up.

Assertiveness and communication go hand-in-hand. Assertiveness means to express feelings in a firm, yet reasonable, way, and to never allow another person to barrel over you with their anger. Don't say yes when it is not what you mean. Assertiveness also never equals becoming mean or aggressive. We teach others how to treat us. When we give in to temper tantrums, we teach others that they can control us that way. When we assert ourselves in a firm yet kind way, others have more respect for us and treat us accordingly.

Seek to communicate in a clear, positive, and assertive way.

8. Rooting for Each Other—Mutual support and praise are essential for healthy relationships. Individuals in relationships thrive when their partners root for them and when their partners show clearly that they want them to come out on top. Unfortunately, many couples compete with each other to find out who is "right" or who is "better." In a close relationship, competition is often destructive.

Craig undermined his wife's attempt to go back to school. Marilyn had often told Craig that she wanted to return to school once their youngest child started kindergarten. She enrolled in a respiratory therapy program at a local community college. She had had asthma as a child and felt she could empathize with people who had breathing problems. When Marilyn had first raised this idea five years before, Craig was supportive. But as the time drew closer, he began making excuses for her not to start the program. He complained about finances, her time away from the family, and said they were doing just fine with her at home. Marilyn felt betrayed by Craig's attitude because he had supported her until it was time to start the program. Marilyn secretly felt that Craig was jealous, because within two years, she would make more money than he brought home after being in his grocery store job for more than fifteen years. Whatever his reasons, it was clear that Craig's attitude placed him in jeopardy of losing Marilyn's respect and love. When a partner feels betrayed it is hard to recapture positive feelings.

Marilyn's sister, Judy, was no help for Craig. She told Marilyn how supportive her husband, Leo, had been when she went back to school. Leo watched the kids, did many chores around the house, and made sure that she had plenty of time to study. Leo was Judy's best supporter. Even when Judy felt overwhelmed and wanted to quit, Leo nudged her along, helping her reach her goal. Judy told Marilyn that when she graduated from college, Leo owned a part of her diploma and that she would always love him for his support.

Between Leo and Craig, who do you think came out the winner? Leo helped his partner feel successful, happy, and fulfilled. He was a part of her success, and Judy appreciated him for it. Craig, on the other hand, was in danger of losing his wife. By choosing the selfish role of maintaining the status quo and attempting to hold Marilyn back, he was in danger of losing his best friend. How good are you at supporting the needs of your partner? Do you consider their goals and desires? Does your partner believe that you are on his or her side? Or is your relationship based on games such as "winners and losers," "who's better," or "who's right"? Try to root for your partner. Keeping your partner's best interest in mind is most often in your best interest. Supporting each others' personal goals is an investment that will pay many dividends.

9. Forgiveness—The ability to forgive is an essential quality in a relationship. People who hold on to injuries from the past ruin their own happiness and damage the relationship. Letting go of past hurts is essential for both personal and relational health. In my experience, people who are angry and unforgiving experience irritability, muscle tension, stomach upset, high blood pressure, and headaches. People who hold on to hurts also go through more friends and lovers than those who are able to let go of unimportant issues.

The cold, hard fact is that we all make mistakes, every single one of us. There is no question that some of us make more mistakes than others, but no one is perfect, at least no one that I have ever met. In therapy with couples, I use the metaphor of "buckets of smelly fish" to represent past hurts and injustices. Most couples who are having trouble carry around their "bucket of smelly fish" almost like war medals, as if the smelly fish are important to them. Whenever there is an argument or disagreement, they take several of the smelly fish out and throw them at each other. Unfortunately, "buckets of smelly fish," or holding on to hurts from the past means that a foul aroma will be in the air most of the time.

The first six years of Jason and Marsha's marriage were good. Then Jason got involved in a business venture with two of his friends. He had put a lot of time and money into the business. When it went sour, Jason and Marsha lost all of their savings and nearly lost their home. Marsha, who grew up with a father who was successful in business, was angry at Jason's failure. She started to question his business judgment and reminded him of the failure whenever he proposed a new project. At first, Jason gave in to his wife's assessment that he was a failure, and he got a secure job working for someone else. But his resentment began to show when he accused Marsha of undermining the attempts he made to get them ahead. "Lots of people fail before they get it right," he said. "One failure means I still have things to learn." It wasn't until they could air these hurts that they were able to get rid of the "smelly fish" that came between them.

Forgiveness does not mean stupidity. Don't stay with people who physically hurt you, who repetitively cheat on you, who repeatedly belittle you, or who never talk to you. Forgiveness does mean letting go of the frailties and mistakes we all make. It means assuming the best about your partner. "Forgive and you will be forgiven," and "Let the person who is without sin cast the first stone," are two of my favorite Biblical verses and are therapeutic to the culture of a relationship.

10. Respect—Respect is often the barometer of the relationship. The higher the level of respect a couple has for each other, the more solid the relationship. Low levels of respect indicate serious trouble. Respect or respectful behavior in a relationship originates from the belief that a partner is "worthy" of high esteem. It is not something that you can expect or demand. Respect is something that evolves over time. It is mutual when it is truly present.

Here are some behaviors that demonstrate respect. Which ones would you add to the list?

- Support each other in difficult parenting situations.
- Be kind and thoughtful toward each other in private and in public.
- Listen to your partner's opinion.
- Be truthful in a kind way, even when it hurts.
- Be on time when you know it is important to your partner.
- Take over chores when you know your partner is feeling down.

Here are some behaviors that demonstrate disrespect. Any additions?

- Discounting your partner's thoughts or ideas
- Talking about your partner behind his or her back
- Not calling when you're going to be late
- Being late to appointments or functions that are important to your partner
- Belittling your partner in front of the children

Mutual respect means:

- Honesty and trust
- Kindness
- Fidelity

- Hope
- Priority
- Friendship
- Clear communication and assertiveness
- Rooting for each other
- Forgiveness

WHAT ARE YOUR VALUES?

Values go hand in hand with principles and culture in a relationship. Values are qualities that you believe are important and hold in high regard. When values coincide, synergy strengthens the relationship; when values are at odds, a tension tears apart the relationship. It is important to understand what each person values in the relationship.

To understand your and your partner's value systems, please answer the following questions:

1. First, rank the following twelve items in order of their importance to you (1 = most important, 12 = least important).

	You	Your Partner
Personal wisdom	_____	_____
Wealth	_____	_____
Fulfilling relationships	_____	_____
Fame	_____	_____
Individual accomplishments	_____	_____
Legacy	_____	_____
Honesty/integrity	_____	_____
Faith in yourself	_____	_____
Faith in a higher power	_____	_____
How you appear to others	_____	_____
Sexuality	_____	_____
Security	_____	_____

2. With the above ranking in mind, what are you now doing to accomplish or enhance the first five items you placed on the list? What is your partner doing?

1. _____

2. _____

3. _____

4. _____

5. _____

3. What additional steps will help to reach your goals? What can your partner do?

1. _____

2. _____

3. _____

4. _____

5. _____

4. Imagine yourself lying in your coffin after your life ends. What has really mattered to you in your life? What had eternal value for you? How would your partner answer this question? (If you don't know, ask!)

5. Are you giving enough time and effort to those people or things that really matter to you? Or are you unconsciously spending the bulk of your time on things of lesser personal value? Again, how would your partner answer this question? (If you don't know, ask!)

Chapter 4

Killing the A.N.T.S in Your Relationship:

Correcting the thoughts that really hurt your relationship

"He never listens to me."

"Just because we had a good weekend doesn't mean anything."

"You don't respect me."

"You're going to cheat on me."

"I felt like you ignored me."

"It's my fault that we have such trouble."

"You're arrogant."

"You're late because you don't care."

"It's your fault."

These are examples of thoughts that severely limit a couple's ability to enjoy their life together. How couples think "moment-by-moment" has a huge impact on how they feel and how they behave in the relationship. Negative thoughts often lead to difficult behaviors and cause most internal "feeling" problems couples have, as well as the external or interpersonal problems. Hopeful thoughts, on the other hand, influence behavior positively and lead couples to feel good about themselves and to be more effective in their relationships.

Total focus requires a person to think in ways that are beneficial to the process of developing a relationship. Unfortunately, we are not taught formally to contemplate the thoughts or challenge the notions that go through our minds, even though our thoughts are always with us. Why do we spend so much time having teenagers memorize geometry theorems and so little time teaching them how to think clearly? Most people do not understand the significance of thoughts, and they leave the development of thought patterns to chance. Did you know that thoughts have actual weight and mass? They are real! They influence every cell in your body. When your mind is burdened with many negative thoughts, it affects your ability to learn, your ability to relate to other people, and your physical health. Teaching couples to control their thoughts in a positive direction is one of the most effective ways to help a couple repair their relationship.

Here are some of the positive-thinking principles that I use in my psychotherapy practice with couples. When couples learn these principles they gain more control over their feelings and their behavior.

PRINCIPLE #1

Did you know... every time you have a thought, your brain releases chemicals? That's how our brains work.

You have a thought. Your brain releases chemicals. An electrical transmission moves across your brain. You become aware of what you're thinking.

Thoughts are real and have a real impact on how you feel and how you behave.

PRINCIPLE #2

Every time you have an angry, unkind thought, a sad or a cranky thought, your brain releases negative chemicals that make your body feel bad. Think about the last time you were mad. How did your body react? When people are angry, often their muscles tense, their hearts beat faster, their hands start to sweat, and they may even begin to feel a little dizzy. Your body reacts to every negative thought you have.

PRINCIPLE #3

Every time you have a good, happy thought, hopeful or kind thought, your brain releases chemicals that make your body feel good. Think about the last time you had a really happy thought. How did your body feel? When people are happy their muscles relax, their hearts beat slower, their hands become dry, and they breathe slower. Your body also reacts to your good thoughts.

PRINCIPLE #4

Your body reacts to every thought that you have. We know this from polygraphs, or lie-detector tests. During a lie-detector test, you are hooked up to some fancy equipment that measures:

- hand temperature
- heart rate
- blood pressure
- breathing rate
- muscle tension
- how much the hands sweat

The tester then asks questions such as, "Did you do that thing?" If you did the thing (and it was a bad thing), your body is likely to have a stress response, and it is likely to react in the following ways:

- hands get colder
- heart beats faster
- blood pressure rises
- breathing gets faster
- muscles tighten
- hands sweat more

Almost immediately, your body reacts to what you think, whether you say anything or not. The opposite is also true. If you did not do the thing they are asking you about, it is likely that your body would experience a relaxation response and react in the following ways:

- hands become warmer

- heart rate slows
- blood pressure drops down
- breathing becomes slower and deeper
- muscles relax more
- hands become drier

Again, almost immediately, your body reacts to what you think. This not only happens when you are asked about telling the truth, your body reacts to every thought you have, whether it relates to work, friends, family, or anything else.

PRINCIPLE #5

Thoughts are powerful. They can make your mind and your body feel good or they can make you feel bad. Every cell in your body is affected by every thought you have. That is why when people get emotionally upset they actually develop physical symptoms, such as headaches or stomachaches. Some people believe that individuals who think a lot of negative thoughts are more likely to get cancer. If you can think about good things, you will feel better.

Abraham Lincoln had periods of serious depression when he was a child and young adult. He considered killing himself and had days when he didn't even get out of bed. Later in his life, however, he learned to treat his bad feelings with laughter. He became a good storyteller and loved to tell jokes. He learned that when he laughed, he felt better. More than a hundred years ago, some people recognized how important thoughts were in relation to our physical health.

Think of your body as an ecosystem. An ecosystem contains an entire environment: the water, the land, the cars, the people, the animals, the vegetation, the houses, the landfills. A negative thought, then, would be like pollution to your system. Just as pollution in the Los Angeles Basin affects everyone who goes outside, so too do negative thoughts pollute your mind and your body.

PRINCIPLE # 6

Unless you monitor your thoughts, they are automatic or they "just happen." Thoughts that just happen are not necessarily correct. Your thoughts are not always the truth. Sometimes you even lie to yourself. I treated a college student who thought he was stupid because he didn't do well on tests. When he took an IQ test, however, we discovered that he was near-genius in intelligence! You don't have to believe every thought that passes through your head. It is important to consider whether your thoughts help you or hurt you. If you never challenge your thoughts, you just believe them as if they were true.

PRINCIPLE #7

You can train yourself to think positively and hopefully, or you can just allow your negative thoughts to upset you. Once you learn how to control your thoughts, you can choose to think good thoughts and feel good, or you can choose to think bad thoughts and feel lousy. It's up to you. You can learn how to change your thoughts, and you can learn to change the way you feel.

One way to learn how to change your thoughts is to recognize when they are negative and talk back to them. If you can correct negative thoughts, you take away their power over you. When you don't challenge a negative thought, your mind believes it is true and your body reacts to it.

PRINCIPLE #8

As I just mentioned, negative thoughts are mostly automatic or "just happen." I call these thoughts "automatic negative thoughts (or a.n.t.s). Think of these negative thoughts that invade your mind like ants at a picnic. One negative thought, like one ant at a picnic, is not a problem. Two or three negative thoughts, like two or three ants at a picnic, become more irritating. Ten or twenty negative thoughts, like ten or twenty ants at a picnic, may ruin the picnic. Whenever you notice automatic negative thoughts or a.n.t.s, you should crush them, or they could ruin your relationships. One way to crush these a.n.t.s is to write them down and respond to them. For example, if you think "My husband never listens to me," write the thought down. Then write down a rational response, something like, "He's not listening to me now... maybe he's distracted by something else. He often listens to me." When you write down negative thoughts and talk back to them, you remove their power and help yourself feel better. Some people tell me they have trouble talking back to negative thoughts because they feel as though they are lying to themselves. Initially, they believe that the thoughts that go through their mind are the truth. Remember, your thoughts are sometimes lies. It is important to check them out before you simply believe them!

Here are nine different types of thoughts that can make situations out to be worse than they are. Think of these nine types as different species. When you identify the type of a.n.t., you begin to take away the power it has over you. I have designated some of these a.n.t.s as red, because they are particularly harmful. Recognize and exterminate a.n.t.s whenever possible.

A.N.T. #1:
"ALWAYS" THINKING

When you think something that happened will always repeat itself, you are stuck in "always" thinking. For example, if your partner is irritable and gets upset, you might think to yourself, "She's always yelling at me," even though she yells only once in a while. But just the thought, "She's always yelling at me," is so negative that it makes you feel sad and upset. Whenever your thoughts contain words such as "always," "never," "no one," "everyone," "every time," "everything," you are engaged in "always" thinking. Such thinking is *usually wrong*. Many examples of "always" thinking arise in a relationship, such as "He's always putting me down" or "She's never interested in making love." "Always" a.n.t.s are common. Watch out for them.

A.N.T. #2 (RED A.N.T.): FOCUSING ON THE NEGATIVE

This occurs when you *only see the bad* in a situation and ignore anything good that might happen. For example, what if you had to move? Naturally, you would be sad to leave your friends, but would you not think of the new places you would see and the new friends you would make? It is important to focus on the good parts of your life rather than the bad.

I once treated a man who was depressed. When our sessions began, he could only think about the bad things that had happened to him. He had recently moved to my city, and he told me that he would never have friends (even though he already had several); he also said he would do poorly in his new job (even though his initial evaluation was good); and he said he would never have any fun (even though he had joined a local tennis club). By focusing on the negative in his new situation, he was making it hard for himself to adjust to his new home. He would have been much better off if he had focused on all the positive aspects of his situation rather than the negative ones.

Negative people can learn a powerful lesson from the Disney movie *Pollyanna*. In the movie, Pollyanna goes to live with her aunt after her missionary parents die. Even though she had lost her parents, she was eventually able to help many people with her positive attitude. She introduced them to the "glad game," which was to look for things to be glad about in any situation. Her father had taught her the game after she had experienced a disappointment. She had always wanted a doll, but her parents never had had enough money to buy it for her. Her father had sent a request for a secondhand doll to his missionary sponsors. By mistake, they sent her a pair of crutches. "What is there to be glad about, getting crutches?" they asked. Then they decided they could be glad because they didn't have to use them. The minister was especially affected by Pollyanna. Before she arrived in town, he preached hellfire and damnation, and he seemed unhappy. Pollyanna told him that her father had said that the Bible had eight hundred "glad passages," and that if God mentioned being glad that many times, it must be because God wants us to think that way. Focusing on the negative in a situation will make you feel bad. Playing the glad game, or looking for the positive, will help you feel better.

A.N.T. #3 (RED A.N.T.)
FORTUNE-TELLING:

This is where you predict the worst possible outcome to a situation. For example, before you discuss an important issue with your partner, you predict that he or she won't be interested in what you have to say. Just thinking this will make you feel tense. I call fortune-telling a red a.n.t., because sometimes, by predicting bad things, you can make them happen. Say you are driving home from work, and you predict that the house will be a wreck, and no one will be interested in seeing you. By the time you get home, you are ready for a fight. When you see one thing out of place, or no one comes running to the door to greet you, you explode and ruin the rest of the evening. Fortune-telling a.n.t.s can really ruin your chances for feeling good.

A.N.T. #4 (RED A.N.T.)
MIND-READING

When you believe that you know what another person is thinking even when they haven't told you, you are engaging in mind-reading. Many people read minds, (or think they do) and more often than not it gets them into trouble. It is a common cause of trouble between people. I tell my wife, "Please don't read my mind, I have enough trouble reading it myself!" You know that you are trying to mind-read when you have thoughts such as, "She's mad at me," "He doesn't like me," or "They were talking about me." I tell people that a negative look from someone else may mean nothing more than constipation.

You can't read someone else's mind. You never know what they are thinking. To help couples overcome mind-reading a.n.t.s, I teach them the 18/40/60 Rule, which says: When you are 18, you worry about what everyone is thinking of you; when you're 40, you don't give a damn about what anybody is thinking of you; and when you're 60, you realize nobody's been thinking about you at all. People spend their days worrying and thinking about themselves, not you. Think about your day. What have you thought about today? What others (even your partner) are doing, or what you have to do or want to do? Odds are you've been thinking about you. Even in intimate relationships, you cannot read your partner's mind. When you don't understand something, clarify it, but stay away from mind-reading a.n.t.s. They are infectious.

A.N.T. #5
THINKING WITH YOUR FEELINGS:

When you believe your negative feelings without question, you are thinking with your feelings. Feelings are complex and often based on powerful memories. As with your thoughts, feelings are sometimes lies. But many people trust their feelings, though they have no evidence to back them up. Thinking-with-your-feelings thoughts usually start with the words "I feel." For example, "I feel like you don't love me." "I feel stupid." "I feel like a failure." "I feel nobody will ever trust me." Whenever you have a strong negative feeling, check it out. Look for the evidence behind the feeling.

Do you have real reasons to feel that way? Or, are you simply applying feelings from old, inapplicable events or memories to the present circumstances?

A.N.T. #6
GUILT BEATINGS

Guilt is not a helpful emotion, especially for couples. In fact, guilt often causes you to do things that you don't want to do. Guilt beatings occur when your thoughts include words such as "should," "must," "ought," or "have to." Here are some examples: "I ought to spend more time at home." "I must spend more time with my kids." "I should have sex more often." "I have to organize my office." Because of human nature, whenever we think that we "must" do something, no matter what it is, we don't want to do it.

Remember the story of Adam and Eve? The only restriction that God put on them when he gave them the Garden of Eden was that they shouldn't eat from the Tree of Knowledge. Almost immediately after God told them what they shouldn't do, they began to wonder why they shouldn't do it. You know the rest of the story. They ate from the tree and ended up being banned from the Garden of Eden. It is better to replace guilt beatings with phrases like "I want to do this..." "It fits my goals to do that..." "It would be helpful to do this..." So in the negative examples above, it would help to change those phrases to "I want to spend more time at home." "It is in our best interest for my kids and me to spend more time together." "I want to please my spouse by making wonderful love with him (or her) because he (or she) is important to me." "It is in my best interest to organize my office." Get rid of unnecessary emotional turbulence that keeps you from achieving the goals you want.

A.N.T. #7
LABELING

Whenever you attach a negative label to yourself or to someone else, you destroy your ability to look at the situation clearly. Some examples of negative labels that couples use are "jerk," "frigid," "arrogant," and "irresponsible." Negative labels are harmful, because whenever you call yourself or someone else arrogant or a jerk, you have lumped that person with all of the "jerks" or "arrogant people" that you've ever known, and you are no longer able to deal with them in a reasonable way. Avoid negative labels.

A.N.T. #8
PERSONALIZATION

People sometimes take innocuous events personally. "My boss didn't talk to me this morning. He must be mad at me." Or, one feels he or she is the cause of all the bad things that happen. For instance, "My son got into a car accident. I should have spent more time teaching him to drive. It must be my fault." People have many reasons for their behavior besides negative explanations related to you. For example, your boss may not have spoken to you because he was preoccupied, upset, or in a hurry. Since you can never fully know why people do what they do, it is pointless to take their behavior personally.

A.N.T. #9 (THE MOST POISONOUS RED A.N.T.)
BLAME

Many relationships are ruined by people who blame their partners when things go wrong. Such people take little personal responsibility. When something goes wrong at home or at work, they try to find someone to blame, rarely admitting their own role in their problems. Typically, you will hear statements from them such as:

"It wasn't my fault that..."
"That wouldn't have happened if you had..."
"How was I supposed to know..."
"It's your fault that..."

The bottom line statement goes something like this: "If only you had done something differently, then I wouldn't be in the predicament I'm in. It's your fault, and I'm not responsible."

Blaming others starts early in life. I have three children. When my youngest, Katie, was eighteen months old, she would blame her brother, who was eleven, for any trouble she might be in. Her nickname for him was Didi, and "Didi did it," even if he wasn't home. One day she spilled a drink at the table while her mother's back was turned. When her mother turned around and saw the mess, she asked what had happened. Katie told her, "Didi spilled my drink." When her mother told her that her brother was at a friend's house, Katie persisted, "Didi did it."

Whenever you blame someone else for the problems in your life, you become powerless to change anything. Many couples play the "blame game," but it rarely helps them. Avoid blaming thoughts and take personal responsibility for your own problems so that you have the power to solve them.

SUMMARY OF A.N.T. SPECIES:

1. *"Always" thinking:* thinking in words such as "always," "never," "no one," "everyone," "every time," "everything."
2. *Focusing on the negative:* only seeing the bad in a situation.
3. *Fortune-telling:* predicting the worst possible outcome to a situation.
4. *Mind-reading:* believing that you know what another person is thinking even though they haven't told you.

5. *Thinking with your feelings:* believing negative feelings are truth without ever questioning them.
6. *Guilt beatings:* thinking in words such as "should," "must," "ought to," or "have to."
7. *Labeling:* attaching a negative label to yourself or to someone else.
8. *Personalization:* innocuous events are taken to have personal meaning.
9. *Blame:* blaming someone else for the problems you have.

Whenever you notice an a.n.t. entering your mind, train yourself to crush it. Become an expert a.n.t. exterminator or the a.n.t.s will ruin your day. One way to crush these a.n.t.s is to write down the negative thoughts, identify them as a problem, and talk back to them. When you write down automatic negative thoughts and talk back to them, you begin to take away their power and gain control over your moods.

Here are several examples from some of the thoughts at the beginning of this section.

A.N.T.	Species	Kill the A.N.T. (Talk Back)
He never listens to me.	"Always" thinking	That's simply not true. He often listens to me. Tonight he must be preoccupied.
Just because we had a good weekend doesn't mean anything. We'll be fighting again in a few days.	Focusing on the negative	Thank God we had a good weekend. It may be the start of many good days together.

She doesn't respect me.	Mind-reading	Sometimes it feels as though she doesn't respect me, but there are other times when I feel love and respect from her.
You're going to cheat on me.	Fortune-telling	Unless I have evidence, I won't accuse you of something so terrible. I know if I act like a jealous partner, it is more likely to turn you away from me.
I felt like you ignored me.	Thinking with my feelings	I get hurt when you do not pay attention to me when we're out together, but I understand that sometimes you get preoccupied. Next time I'll nudge you when I feel ignored.
You should spend more time with me.	Guilt beatings	It would be helpful for us to spend more time together. I miss you. (Which statement is likely to get you the best response?)

You're arrogant.	Labeling	I have trouble with how confident you are at times. It brings out some of my own insecurity.
You're late because you don't care.	Personalization	I need to check out why you were late before I come to any conclusions.
It's your fault.	Blame	I need to look at my part of the problem and look for ways I can improve the situation.

Your thoughts and the thoughts of your partner matter. Kill the a.n.t.s that come between you. Left unchecked they will cause an infestation that will only grow.

Chapter 5

Principles of Effective Negotiation in Relationships

Negotiation is not a dirty word, nor even a necessary evil. It is a good process. Unfortunately, many people associate negotiation with back-room politicians, Tijuana merchants, or used car salesmen, and they avoid it as if it were something bad. Because they have a negative attitude toward negotiation, many people never learn this valuable skill.

Learning to negotiate, however, can make your daily life and the lives of those around you much more effective. In fact, most people negotiate frequently without ever realizing it. Working out chores, deciding what movie to see or what restaurant to go to, deciding which projects to do first, agreeing about sex, or dealing with the kids are just some everyday examples of negotiation. Developing this skill will be essential for you as you construct your Two-Minute Focus Statement.

This chapter presents fifteen essential negotiation principles with everyday examples of how couples can apply these principles immediately to their lives.

STEP ONE:
ASSUME THE BEST ABOUT YOUR PARTNER UNLESS YOU HAVE CLEAR REASON NOT TO

Assuming the best about your partner is a good starting point in negotiation. When you do this you are able to look out for their welfare as well as your own, which makes the process more effective in the long run. Too often couples start with mistrust or anger, which clouds the whole negotiation process. Believing the best about your partner, unless you have clear reason not to, will help you get what you want.

Personal negotiations are different from political or business negotiation, where both sides may only be out for what they can get. We assume that partners in good relationships (this includes business relationships) want the best for each other, that the relationship is not totally one-sided. Of course, this is not always true, but when you start with that assumption, you're more likely to behave effectively in the relationship, and you are more likely to be able to negotiate in good faith. This is the first principle I teach couples in my practice. These are the "Positive Basic Assumptions" (PBAs) mentioned in Chapter Three. Our behavior is based on our underlying beliefs. When you believe your partner has your best interests in mind, you are more likely to treat them kindly and supportively. When you believe that they are trying to hurt you or that they don't care about you, you will be suspicious and perhaps somewhat hostile, which is likely to hurt the process. Start by assuming the best about your partner.

STEP TWO:
LOOK OUT FOR YOUR INTERESTS
AND YOUR PARTNER'S INTERESTS

Many people have the notion that self-interest is bad, and that people shouldn't negotiate the best for themselves. They believe that working in their own best interest is selfish and makes them an immoral person. Guilt prevents them from getting what they want.

Self-interest is not a bad policy! It is essential to happy relationships. Consider the mother in a family who spends all her time doing things for her husband and kids. On the surface her actions appear selfless and giving. Yet, the mothers I meet who do things for everyone else in their families are not happy people. Instead they are angry and resentful. Their anger spills over and hurts their relationships with their spouse and children. In therapy, I show these women that by doing everything for their husbands and children, they inadvertently have trained them not to be helpful. Because they did not ask for what they needed (help and time for themselves), they made the situation worse rather than better. I then teach them to take back control and get the help they need, which in the long run, is better for everyone involved. Because Mom has more time, she has a more positive attitude.

When I was a psychiatric resident at Walter Reed Army Medical Center in Washington, D.C., the chief of the department used to say, "Everyone is out for themselves. It is just that the more sophisticated they are, the harder it is to tell." To get what you want in life, self-interest is a necessary and valuable principle in negotiation when used in conjunction with understanding and helping others to pursue their needs.

Of course, if you are strictly out for yourself in negotiations, you will have problems. Effective negotiation is a two-way process, and it is essential for both parties to believe that each side will benefit from the interaction. Likewise, in negotiation it is critical for you to be able to understand the other person's perspective so that you can find ways to give them what they want in the context of your needs. "Love your neighbor as yourself" is a rule that will help the negotiation process for couples. You can't love your neighbor if you have little or no love for yourself, and you can't love yourself if you are trying to hurt your neighbor.

STEP THREE:
BE CLEAR ON THE ISSUE OR ISSUES
YOU ARE NEGOTIATING

Clarity is essential in negotiations. One of the reasons relationships get into trouble is that the partners are not discussing or negotiating the same issue. For example, Bill and Judy continually argued over the checkbook, because Judy would never balance it. Bill took that as a sign that she didn't care about their finances. They argued about it every month when Bill wrote out the bills. Finally, when they sat down to negotiate this problem, Bill asked her why she didn't care about their finances. Judy said that she did care, but she was afraid that if she tried to balance the checkbook she would mess it up. When she was single she had had three separate checking accounts that she had had to close because she had managed them so badly. Bill then understood that Judy needed education and training rather than blame. They negotiated a solution in which Bill would train her on the simple computer program he used to balance the checkbook, and she in turn promised to balance her checkbook every two weeks.

STEP FOUR:
GATHER INFORMATION BEFORE
YOU GIVE OUT TOO MUCH

In negotiating anything, it is important to gather as much information as possible before you give out information. This has several advantages, including:

- The other person's starting position may be better than you think;
- The other person may give you information that causes you to change the way you think; or,
- It buys you time to figure out the best position in the negotiation.

Gathering information before you give out any is easier than most people think. It requires two skills: the ability to listen actively and the ability to ask open-ended questions. Active listening is key to gathering information. The principles of active listening are simple. First, repeat what you have heard and wait for the person to continue the conversation. For example, when your partner says, "I want to do things this way..." rather than saying, "No, I don't like that," repeat "You want things done that way?" Then wait for them to continue. More often than not they will give you information that will help you understand the reasons behind their request. Too often, people react to what the other person says before they truly understand the meaning behind what was said.

Asking open-ended questions is also important in negotiations. These include questions that require more information. They are not questions that can be answered with a specific answer or with a yes or no. Examples include, "Can you tell me more about that?" "Say more." "Can you help clarify this point for me?" "Can you tell me the reasons for that thought?"

Here are two ways that Susan and Philip can approach the issue of whether this couple will accept a move Philip's company is offering him. The first example is how many couples negotiate differences; in the second one, Susan uses active listening and open-ended questions to negotiate the conflict.

> **Philip:** My company offered me a job in Nevada.
> **Susan:** I'm not going to Nevada. I don't want to leave my job, leave all my friends, and pull the kids out of school.
> **Philip:** But it is really a good opportunity for me within this company.
> **Susan:** What about us? Don't you care about us?
> **Philip:** Don't you know my job is what pays most of the bills around here? Don't you care about that?

In this example the conversation deteriorates into anger and accusations. Here is the second approach to negotiate the same issue using active listening and asking open-ended questions.

> **Philip:** My company offered me a job in Nevada.
> **Susan:** They offered you a job in Nevada?

(repeating back what she heard and
waiting for Philip to continue)

Philip: It is really a good opportunity for me within
this company.

Susan: Can you tell me more about it?

Philip: I'll get a raise and a promotion.

Susan: That's wonderful. What are your thoughts
about the offer?

Philip: I have mixed feelings. I'm flattered that
they offered me the position, but you have
your job here, we have our friends, and
the kids are doing well in school.

Susan: It's a lot to give up. Do you think it's worth
it?

Philip: I don't know. We will really have to discuss
it and agree on the best course before we
make such a big decision.

The second scenario has a completely different
outcome. Active listening and asking open-ended
questions will make you a much more effective
negotiator.

Effective negotiators are able to get into the heads
of the other person to see what motivates them and to
understand what it is they really want out of the
transaction. They realize that if they can consider the
other person's wants and needs, they are more likely
to be successful. This is why it is important to gather
as much information as possible before stating your
position.

STEP FIVE:
GIVE YOUR POSITION
AND THE REASONS BEHIND IT

After you have gathered as much information as
possible and have taken enough time to study the issues,
clearly state your position on the matter and the reasons
for it. A clear statement on what you want and why you
want it is more likely to get your needs met.

Unfortunately, many people act as though their partners should read their minds. Statements such as, "He should have known..." "It should have been obvious what I wanted..." "If she loved me she would have been able to tell..." are common in relationships, but they are destructive. No one can read your mind. No one! In treating couples, I've found that many play the "guess what's bothering me" game. When one partner senses something is wrong and inquires about it, the other person says, "Nothing is wrong," even though he or she may be slamming cupboards or speaking in a hostile tone. "Guess what's bothering me" is a poor negotiating tool. When you want something in a relationship, tell your partner.

Sam owned a small business that was going through tough times. He wanted his girlfriend Jill to become more involved in the business to help save money. He never came out and said what he wanted. He just complained about his problems, hoping she would take the hint. When she didn't, he blurted out that she didn't care about his needs. Jill was confused. They fought. When the air cleared Jill told Sam she would be happy to help him in the business, as long as he promised that the next time he would just ask her directly.

STEP SIX:
FIND AREAS OF COMMON GROUND

After both sides have clearly stated their positions, it is important to look for areas of common ground. Finding common ground is critical to successful negotiations. To find this position, it is necessary to understand both your and your partner's needs. It is also important to know what is really important to you and what you are willing to give up. Preparation is essential for this step.

I have good friends who live in New York City. They decided to move to a different part of Manhattan to be in between their places of work. Ted wanted to live in a boxy place that had a lot of services (parking garage, gymnasium, security guard, etc.). When he told Ann his idea, she protested, saying she wanted to live in a cute home that she could decorate and make her own. Ted was not interested in cute; he wanted services. After several days, Ann said she would go for a place with lots of services if she could have a home with space, light, and a view. They were able to find a place with the services Ted wanted that also had lots of space, a wonderful view, and windows that captured plenty of light.

Common ground may take some negotiation, but with good communication it can almost always be found. It is necessary to know what is not important to you in the discussions. Be clear about what you want, but also be willing to trade off less important areas when needed.

STEP SEVEN: IDENTIFY THE MAJOR DIFFERENCES

In difficult negotiations, you may discover major differences in what you are willing to accept and what is offered. It is important early in negotiations to identify the potential obstacles and search for ways around them. If you recognize them early, you may have more time for creative problem-solving. Examples of major differences in relationships might include issues of religion, whether or not to have children, sexual expression, and handling finances.

Some couples hide these issues in the closet until one day they explode into turmoil. George and Carol disagreed on whether or not to have children. George, forty-two, was an only child and was focused on his career. Carol, thirty-seven, who also had a successful career, felt that her biological clock was ticking down. When they dated, George said he didn't want children; he felt his career would not allow him the time that children needed. Carol, not wanting to alienate George, kept her desires quiet. But now she felt panicked. She cried at the beginning of every menstrual period, and sex between them became mechanical and tense. They almost split up over the issue. In therapy, George said that he would have still married Carol if he had known she wanted children, but now he felt she had backed him into a corner and had gone against their agreement. That troubled him. It is important to speak the truth and identify major differences early in a relationship.

STEP EIGHT: CLARIFY THE DEAL KILLERS

Likewise, couples must identify "deal killers" in their relationships. "Deal killers" are issues that end the negotiations or terminate the relationship. Spelling these out up front will help give direction to the relationship. For example, many people tell themselves that if their partner has an affair, they will leave the relationship. If that is the case, it is important to communicate that to your partner. Physical abuse, financial dishonesty, affairs, and alcoholism are examples of deal killers in relationships.

When I was in the military, I was the medical consultant for the drug and alcohol treatment program at the post where I was stationed. One of the most effective interventions with young alcoholic men that I witnessed occurred when their wives told them that if they didn't stop drinking, they would leave them. When the wife took that position early in the man's alcohol abuse, the men were more likely to stop drinking completely. The soldier got the clear message that his alcohol intake threatened the marriage and that he needed to choose between drinking excessive amounts of alcohol and being married. If the woman vacillated on this issue, perhaps because of her own dependency needs or feelings of insecurity, the man was much less likely to stop his destructive alcoholic behavior. Clarifying deal killers up front goes a long way to preventing them.

STEP NINE:
BEING PROACTIVE AND DOING SOMETHING IS NOT ALWAYS BETTER THAN DOING NOTHING

Sometimes people become anxious in negotiations and feel they must do something to solve a problem or break an impasse. The anxiety and discomfort they feel when a solution is up in the air seems more than they can bear. It is better sometimes, however, to wait for the solution rather than forcing something to happen. When people feel pressured to do something, they are more likely to make mistakes.

Donald and Roberta were in the middle of a heated discussion over Donald's work schedule. Roberta felt that Donald cared more about work than her. She wanted him home more. Donald felt he was at a critical point in his career and wanted more patience and understanding from Roberta. When it became clear to Roberta that they were not going to agree on this issue, she said she thought they should separate. "I want your answer now!" she said. Feeling backed into a corner, Donald packed his things and left. Neither one of them had thought about separating before that evening. But when Roberta felt stuck, she took action to break the impasse, which had an unexpected and unfortunate result. It probably would have been better to table the discussion for a couple of days and look at the situation in a fresh light later on. Having allowed the unconscious mind to work on alternative solutions for a day or two, many people are amazed at the different solutions they come up with. Power plays (such as the one Roberta used) often backfire.

STEP TEN:
CHARACTERIZE GOOD-FAITH OFFERS

When a person makes a genuine offer to compromise, it is important to characterize it that way. Letting another person know that you believe they are sincere and making a good-faith effort to solve the differences will add goodwill to the process and help it along. For example, if you disagree over who does specific chores at home and your partner comes up with an equitable list, note and appreciate his or her effort. You can, of course, give your own input, but only after you compliment them on their initiative. It is important in any relationship to notice sincere behavior and reinforce it with positive comments or gestures. When you never notice or appreciate positive behavior or good faith negotiating, you are not likely to get much of it.

STEP ELEVEN:
MAKE SURE YOUR CARDS ARE ON THE TABLE... NO HIDDEN AGENDAS

When both parties put their cards on the table, the negotiations begin positively. The program is geared toward helping people accomplish this clearly and efficiently. Throughout this process, it is critical to avoid hidden agendas. Hidden agendas, manipulation, and deceit will almost always ruin negotiations. The other party will feel that they cannot trust you, and the negotiations are likely to break down.

Hidden agendas come in many forms. They may masquerade as goodwill gestures, helplessness, or anger. What may appear as goodwill gestures in a relationship may be nothing more than a cover for other behavior. For example, if a husband wants to play golf for the weekend with his buddies, he may offer to send his wife and kids to grandma's house under the pretense of claiming he has to work all weekend (work at hitting a tiny temperamental ball), and he doesn't want them to have to sit at home. If the wife catches his lie, her heightened level of mistrust may permanently color the relationship.

Helplessness is a common ploy in negotiations. When a partner argues that they are unable to do a certain task, it may not be because they really can't do it. Many people use helplessness to get their way...

"You do it so much better than I do..." "I never get it right; please do it..." Illness is a helpless ploy sometimes used to gain power in negotiations... "I'm too sick to do that..." "My back hurts too much..." "I have a headache..."

Anger is another example of a tool people use to promote their hidden agendas. Sometimes people get mad at their partners as an excuse to get out of the house or to get out of doing something they don't want to do. For example, if the husband wants to visit his parents, but the wife has trouble with her mother-in-law, she may start a fight and then refuse to go.

Watch out for hidden agendas. They sabotage negotiations.

STEP TWELVE: ALLOW YOUR MIND TO BE OPEN TO NEW SOLUTIONS

Relationships often get into trouble because people get stuck in old patterns of behavior. In negotiations it is important to have an open mind and to look for creative solutions. When you feel bogged down in an issue, spend some time brainstorming with your partner. List all of the possible solutions no matter how crazy or way out they sound. Initially, don't judge, accept, or reject any of them. You never know what associations even ridiculous solutions might trigger. Our brains work primarily through associations, where one thing leads to another. Writing down all of the possibilities may open up new avenues of thought.

Gail and Richard would frequently get stuck on ways to deal with their families during the holidays. Gail's family pressured her to spend time with them. Richard's family, who lived about three hundred miles away, argued that since they didn't see Richard and Gail in between holidays, they should spend most holidays with them. Both Gail and Richard were baffled by the problem. So, it seemed, every year they fought about what to do. After they learned about brainstorming, they listed seven different solutions to their problem:

- alternating years for each holiday
- spending all the holidays with one family each year and never seeing the other family
- moving to another country so they won't have to deal with the problem
- spending more time with Richard's family during the summer to lessen the pressure at holiday time
- inviting both families over to their house and staying home
- separately visiting their own families during the holidays

Gail and Richard's brainstorming session gave them options to negotiate. They easily eliminated the options of splitting up at holiday time and moving to another country. They settled on a combination of spending more time with Richard's family during the summer and alternating each holiday. They also decided to spend every third holiday at home and invite their families to their house.

STEP THIRTEEN: SEEK THE ADVICE OF OTHERS

When your negotiations bog down, it can be helpful to seek the advice of others who have gone through similar situations. Some people are too proud to ask for help, but that is truly their loss. Why not learn from the mistakes others have made?

I see many couples who have difficult children. Frequently in these situations, the mother complains that the father is too harsh and too distant, and the father complains that the mother doesn't follow through and allows the child to get away with horrid behavior. By seeking outside help from a professional, they can learn new skills and negotiate a more effective strategy, which might be for the father to be kinder to the child and the mother to be firmer with the child. Both parents express an element of truth in the situation, and both parents need to change. Getting outside help or the advice of others can save you many fights and hours of heartache.

STEP FOURTEEN:
DON'T MAKE EVERY ISSUE LIFE OR DEATH

Unless an issue is a "deal-killer" or tremendously dear to your heart, it's important to have the posture of flexibility. When people care too much about a particular issue, they give away all their bargaining power and leverage. The other person knows how badly you want something and is in a position to make you pay dearly for it.

For example, if you are the person in a relationship who desires sex a lot more than the other person and you vocalize this desire loudly, you relinquish your power on this issue. You can become at the mercy or whim of your partner. Don't make any issue so important that you can't negotiate on it. Try to have few critical issues in the negotiations. Don't care about every issue as though it were life or death. You'll have no power in the negotiation.

STEP FIFTEEN:
THE PROCESS IS NEVER ENDING

In a relationship, negotiations occur all the time. The negotiation process is never-ending. The process has no clear beginning and no clear end. Even after decisions are made, it is important to monitor and revise the solutions as the situations change. Use the principles outlined above to be more effective in getting what you want while seeking ways to help your partner get what they want and need.

SUMMARY OF NEGOTIATION STEPS IN RELATIONSHIPS

Step One: Assume the best about your partner unless you have clear reason not to.

Step Two: Look out for your interests and your partner's.

Step Three: Be clear on the issue or issues you are negotiating.

Step Four: Gather information before you give out too much.

Step Five: Give your position and the reasons behind it.

Step Six: Find areas of common ground.

Step Seven: Identify the major differences.

Step Eight: Clarify the deal-killers.

Step Nine: Being proactive and doing something is not always better than doing nothing.

Step Ten: Characterize good-faith offers.

Step Eleven: Make sure your cards are on the table... no hidden agendas.

Step Twelve: Allow your mind to be open to new solutions.

Step Thirteen: Seek the advice of others.

Step Fourteen: Don't make every issue life or death.

Step Fifteen: The process is never ending.

Chapter 6

The Interference of Emotional Problems on Total Focus:

Anxiety disorders, depression, alcohol and drug abuse, adult children of alcoholics, attention deficit disorder, PMS

Late at night several years ago I received a phone call from a close friend who was on the verge of divorce. His wife told him that she couldn't stand the person he had become. When we lived near each other, he was energetic, positive, outgoing, funny, and fascinated by the world around him. As I listened to him on the phone, however, his voice was flat, and he expressed negative thoughts. He told me his life had no meaning, and he would rather die than struggle through another day. My friend was sleeping a lot, had problems concentrating, was irritable and had even lost interest in sex, which was a real change for him. He was the last person in the world with whom I expected to be having that kind of conversation. As I listened to him, I realized he was suffering from clinical depression. The depression was tearing up his marriage. He needed treatment, not a divorce.

Every day in my office, I see emotional or mental problems interfere with a couple's chance for happiness. Too often, couples are blind-sided by illnesses they don't understand, and their relationship is placed in jeopardy. Understanding when mental illness or emotional problems interfere with a relationship is essential to heading off trouble.

Mental illness is extremely common. A recent study by the National Institutes of Mental Health demonstrated that 48 percent of the population will suffer from a mental illness during some point in their lives. Anxiety problems, depression, attention deficit disorders, and alcohol or drug abuse are the most common problems. Mental illnesses strike the rich and the poor, the successful and the not so successful. They devastate individuals and families, and they most often go untreated because of the stigma our society attaches to them. My friend had postponed calling me for more than nine months. He called me only when his wife threatened to divorce him.

Many uninformed people believe erroneously that people with emotional illnesses are strange, scary, or way out. It is true that some people with mental illnesses have delusions or are violent, but the vast majority of people who suffer from anxiety, depression, or drug use are more like you and me than they are different.

If you, your spouse, or your significant other has persistent symptoms, it is important to have a psychiatric evaluation by a competent professional. Too often, because of the stigma, it takes a broken marriage, a job loss, or a life at the brink of suicide before a person seeks help. Our society needs to think of emotional problems in the same light as we think of medical problems so that we can teach emotionally distraught people to seek help, just as they would do if they found blood in their urine.

Here are the six most common emotional problems that I see in my office and their effects on relationships. When left untreated, these problems seriously undermine a person's ability to maintain a relationship. The problems include anxiety disorders, depression, alcohol and drug abuse, growing up in an alcoholic or dysfunctional family, attention deficit disorders, and premenstrual syndrome (PMS).

THE PARALYSIS OF FEAR: ANXIETY DISORDERS

Four common types of anxiety disorders can affect a relationship: panic disorders, agoraphobia, obsessive-compulsive disorders, and post-traumatic stress disorders. I'll briefly discuss each of these to help you recognize symptoms in yourself or your partner so that you can obtain further information.

Panic Disorders: All of a sudden your heart starts to pound. You feel incredible dread. Your breathing rate goes up. You start to sweat. Your muscles tighten. Your hands feel like ice. Your mind starts to race about every terrible thing that could possibly happen and you feel as though you are going to lose your mind if you don't get out of your current situation. You have just had a panic attack.

Panic attacks are one of the most common psychiatric symptoms. Approximately 6 to 7 percent of adults will at some point in their lives suffer from recurrent panic attacks. The attacks often begin in late adolescence or early adulthood but may occur spontaneously later in life. If a person has three attacks in a three-week period, psychiatrists make a diagnosis of a panic disorder.

In a typical panic attack, a person has at least four of the following twelve symptoms: shortness of breath, pounding heart, chest pain, choking or smothering feelings, dizziness, tingling of hands or feet, feeling unreal, hot or cold flashes, sweating, faintness, trembling or shaking, and a fear of dying or going crazy. When the panic attacks first start, many people end up in an emergency room because they think they are having a heart attack. Some people are even admitted to the hospital.

Anticipation anxiety is one of the most difficult symptoms for a person who has a panic disorder. People who suffer from this are often extremely skilled at predicting the worst in situations. In fact, it is often the anticipation of a bad event that brings on a panic attack. For example, you go to the grocery store to do your weekly shopping and you begin to worry that you are going to have an anxiety attack and pass out on the floor. Then, you predict, everyone in the store will look at you and laugh. Soon the symptoms begin. Sometimes a panic disorder can become so severe that a person begins to avoid almost any situation outside of their house—a condition called agoraphobia.

Panic attacks can occur for a variety of reasons. Sometimes they are caused by physical illnesses, such as hyperthyroidism, which is why it is always important to have a physical examination and screening blood work. Sometimes panic attacks can be triggered by excessive caffeine intake or by alcohol withdrawal. Hormonal changes also seem to play a role. Panic attacks in women are seen more frequently at the end of their menstrual cycle, after having a baby, or during menopause. Traumatic events from the past that somehow are sparked unconsciously also can precipitate a series of attacks. Commonly, a person has a family history of panic attacks, alcohol abuse, or other mental illnesses.

Panic disorders can cause many problems in a relationship. If the partner does not understand, he or she might think the person is just trying to avoid unpleasant situations and that the panic disorder is just an excuse or willful behavior. At times, the person with the panic disorder will appear angry, irritable, and irrational, causing their partner to react with dismay, anger, or frustration. Understanding this disorder and its impact on relationships is key to effective treatment.

Agoraphobia: Agoraphobia is a Greek word meaning "fear of the marketplace." In psychiatric terms, agoraphobia is the fear of being alone in public places. The underlying worry is that the person will lose control or become incapacitated and no one will be there to help.

People afflicted with this phobia begin to avoid being in crowds, in stores, or on busy streets. They are often afraid of being in tunnels, on bridges, in elevators, or on public transportation. They usually insist that a family member or a friend accompany them when they leave home. If the fear is imbedded in the person, it may affect his or her entire life. Normal activities become increasingly restricted as the fears or avoidance behaviors dominate this individual's life.

Agoraphobic symptoms often begin in the late teen years or early twenties, but I have seen them start when a person is in his or her fifties or sixties. Often without knowing what is wrong, people try to medicate themselves with excessive amounts of alcohol or drugs. This illness occurs more frequently in women, and many who suffer from it experienced significant separation anxiety as children. Additionally, their family history may include excessive anxiety, panic attacks, depression, or alcohol abuse.

Agoraphobia often evolves out of panic attacks that seem to occur "out of the blue" for no apparent reason. These attacks are so frightening that the agoraphobic begins to avoid any situation that may be associated with the fear. I believe these initial panic attacks are often triggered by unconscious events or anxieties from the past. For example, one of my patients had been raped when she was a teenager in a park late at night. When she was twenty-eight, she had her first panic attack while with her husband in a park late at night. It was the late-night park setting that she associated with the fear of being raped and that triggered the panic attack.

Agoraphobia affects a relationship in many ways. The chronic anxiety associated with agoraphobia causes irritability, tiredness, and a low libido in many of its sufferers. Partners of people with this disorder often don't understand what is happening, and they may take the behavior as a personal insult. Agoraphobia, like the rest of these illnesses, has broken up many relationships. Since many people do not see this problem as a medical illness, they never seek treatment. I treated one woman who had not left her house for forty years. Her husband left her after ten years, and her sister and brother took care of her. Within several months, she responded to a combination of medication and psychotherapy.

Agoraphobia is a frightening illness for the patient and his or her family. With effective, early intervention, however, there is significant hope for recovery.

Obsessive-Compulsive Disorders: On the surface, Gail appeared normal. She went to work every day, she was married to her high school sweetheart, and she had two small children. Inside, Gail felt like a mess. Her husband was ready to leave her, and her children were often withdrawn and upset. Gail was removed from her family because she was locked in the private hell of an obsessive-compulsive disorder. She cleaned her house for hours every night after work. She screamed at her husband and children when anything was out of place. She became especially hysterical if she saw a hair on the floor, and she washed her hands often. She also made her husband and children wash their hands more than ten times a day.

Obsessive-compulsive disorder (OCD) affects somewhere between two and four million people in the U.S. This disorder, almost without exception, dramatically impairs a person's ability to function and often affects the whole family. OCD is often a secret to the outside world, but not to those who live with the person.

The hallmarks of this disorder are obsessions (recurrent, upsetting, or frightening thoughts) or compulsions (behaviors that a person knows make no sense but feels compelled to do anyway). The obsessive thoughts are usually senseless, repugnant, and invade consciousness. They may involve repetitive thoughts of violence (such as killing one's child), contamination (such as becoming infected by shaking hands), or doubt (such as having hurt someone in a traffic accident even though no such accident occurred). The sufferer makes many efforts to suppress or resist these thoughts, but the more a person tries to control them the more powerful the thoughts.

The most common compulsions involve hand-washing, counting, checking, and touching. These behaviors are often performed according to certain rules in a strict or rigid manner. For example, a person with a counting compulsion may feel the need to count every crack on the pavement on their way to work or school. A five-minute walk for most people could turn into a three- or four-hour trip for the person with obsessive-compulsive disorder. They are plagued internally by an urgent, insistent sense of "I have to do it." A part of the individual generally recognizes the senselessness of the behavior and doesn't get pleasure from carrying it out, although doing it releases tension.

The intensity of OCD varies widely. Some people have mild versions, where, for example, they have to have the house perfect before they go on vacation, or they spend the vacation worrying about the condition of the house. The more serious forms can cause a person to be housebound for years. I treated an eighty-three-year-old woman who had obsessive, sexual thoughts that made her feel dirty. It got to the point where she locked all her doors, drew all the window shades, turned off the lights, took the phone off the hook, and sat in the middle of a dark room trying to catch the abhorrent sexual thoughts as they came into her mind. Her behavior paralyzed her life, and she required hospitalization.

OCD can severely affect a person's sexuality. One of my male OCD patients had a difficult time with anything messy. Sexual intercourse upset him because of the stickiness involved. He couldn't get the "mess" out of his mind while making love with his partner. He started avoiding any physical contact with his wife for fear it would lead to intercourse. He had never communicated this obsession to his wife, and she thought he just didn't love her anymore.

Some exciting research using a nuclear medicine study (SPECT) that measures blood flow to the brain has indicated that an overactive area of the brain's frontal lobes may cause some OCD cases. The top middle portion of the frontal lobes allows a person to shift his or her attention from subject to subject. When this area is overactive, a person gets stuck on the same thought or behavior.

Like most forms of mental illness, OCD has a biological basis, and part of effective treatment usually involves medication. Two medications, clomipramine (Anafranil) and fluoxetine (Prozac), have provided many patients with profound relief from OCD symptoms. In addition, behavior therapy is often helpful for these patients. During such therapy, a patient is gradually exposed to the situations most likely to bring out the rituals and habits. Behavior techniques also include thought-stopping and encouragement from the therapist for the patient to face their worst fear (for example, asking a patient with a dirt or contamination fear to play in the mud).

If you have OCD symptoms or know someone who does, it is important to seek early treatment. The longer this illness continues the more entrenched it becomes and the harder it is to treat. The person with OCD and their family are often held hostage by this illness. Anxiety, tension, and "things having to be just so" often cause so much frustration that the family is in danger of breaking apart.

Post-Traumatic Stress Disorders: Joanne, a thirty-four-year-old travel agent, was held up in her office at gunpoint by two men. Four or five times during the robbery, one of the men held a gun to her head and said he was going to kill her. She graphically imagined her brain splattering against the wall. Near the end of this fifteen-minute ordeal, they forced her to remove all her clothes. She pictured them raping her brutally, though they never actually touched her sexually.

Since that time her life had been a turmoil. She

always felt tense. She had flashbacks and nightmares of the robbery. Her stomach was in knots and she had a constant headache. Whenever she went out, she felt panicky. She was frustrated that she could not calm her body: her heart raced, she was short of breath, and her hands were cold and sweaty. She hated the way she felt, and she was angry that her nice life had been turned into a nightmare. What upset her most was that the robbery had affected her marriage and her child. Her baby had picked up her tension and was often fussy. Every time she tried to make love with her husband, she began to cry and got flashbacks of the men raping her.

Joanne was experiencing symptoms of post-traumatic stress disorder (PTSD). PTSD is a psychological reaction to severe traumatic events such as a robbery, rape, car accident, earthquake, tornado, or even a volcanic eruption. Her symptoms were classic for PTSD, especially the flashbacks and nightmares of the event.

Perhaps the worst symptoms, however, came from the horrible thoughts she had during the robbery, such as seeing her brain splattered against the wall and being raped, rather than from what actually happened. These thoughts were registered in her subconscious as fact, and until she entered treatment, she was unable to recognize how much damage they had been doing to her. For example, when she imagined that she was being raped, a part of her began to believe that she actually was raped. The first time she had her period after the robbery, she cried because she was relieved that she was not pregnant by robbers though they had never touched her. A part of her even believed she was dead because she had so vividly pictured her own death.

A significant portion of her treatment was geared toward erasing these erroneous subconscious conclusions. The treatment included hypnotic exercises in which she repeated over and over to herself that she was indeed alive and had not been raped. She was helped to focus on how fortunate she was to escape the horrible events so that she could continue to enjoy her husband and watch her daughter grow up.

Post-traumatic stress disorder has a serious effect on a person's life and can ruin relationships. In Joanne's case she was unable to make love with her husband, she was an emotional wreck, and she was unable to work. Getting treatment is essential for recovery.

Depression: Joseph, a forty-nine-year-old engineer, had been different from his normal self for more than a year. He was irritable, restless, and angry. He alienated several of his friends with his quick temper. Joseph's problems peaked, however, when he physically attacked his wife of twenty-two years during an argument. Joseph had never before struck his wife and, almost immediately thereafter, he realized his life was out of control and he sought treatment.

Sally, a thirty-two-year-old mother of three, had stopped cleaning the house, cooking meals, or taking care of her own appearance. She slept thirteen or more hours a day and always felt tired. She was no longer interested in her hobbies, her kids' activities, or sex with her husband, all of which were dramatic changes from her normal behavior. Her children were bewildered, and her husband was often angry at her.

Joseph and Sally had one thing in common: they both suffered from clinical depression. Depression is a common illness, affecting between twelve and fifteen million Americans annually. Unfortunately, because depression has several different clinical presentations, it often goes unrecognized and untreated. Only a small percentage of people who suffer from depression get adequate treatment.

Symptoms of depression include:
- sad, blue mood
- low energy
- irritability
- decreased concentration
- poor memory
- lack of motivation
- decreased interest in usually pleasurable activities

- lack of sexual interest
- sleep changes, increased or decreased
- appetite changes, increased or decreased
- feelings of helplessness, hopelessness, or worthlessness
- inappropriate guilt
- suicidal thoughts

Many people who know someone who is depressed wish they would "snap out of it," believing that these people have control over how they feel. Nothing could be more wrong. Depression is a biological/medical illness. Over the past several years, metabolic brain studies have shown that depression involves abnormal activity in a person's limbic system (the part of the brain that controls emotions and motivation) and frontal lobes (the part of the brain that controls concentration, judgment, critical thinking, and impulse control).

Depression is a treatable illness. More than 90 percent of people who receive good treatment get significantly better. Without treatment, however, some people's lives are ruined. Their marriage may end in divorce, they may end up being fired from their job, or they may drop out of school. They may even be arrested for a crime after becoming violent. Effective treatment for depression often involves the use of antidepressant medication and psychotherapy.

Since the negative press about the antidepressant Prozac, more people are hesitant to take these medications for depression. This is truly unfortunate. What reporters did not print was that Prozac is the most widely prescribed antidepressant in the world. It was on the cover of *Newsweek* in 1989 as a miracle drug, because many people in state institutions who had not improved on any other medication got significantly better on Prozac. A small percentage of people do become worse, but that is true with all medications. No one should take a medication unless they are closely supervised by their physician. In my clinical experience, Prozac is safe, effective, and often works faster than many of the other antidepressants available.

Even with treatment, it is important to note that depression tends to be recurrent. About two-thirds of people who suffer from a significant depression will experience another episode at some point later in their lives. Knowing the signs and symptoms is essential to getting good care early.

AN ALTERED BRAIN: DRUG AND ALCOHOL ABUSE

Alcohol and drug abuse affect between 5 and 10 percent of the population. In relationships, many people complain that a partner who abuses alcohol or drugs is emotional, erratic, selfish, and unpredictable. In my practice I have seen many relationships fail because of substance abuse. Besides relationship, job, financial, and social problems, the list of health problems associated with alcohol and drug use fill volumes of books. Suffice it to say many of these substances poison your system. Using them is a form of voluntary self-destruction to your body and relationships.

The most common relationship problems associated with substance abuse include guilt, anger, irritability, social withdrawal, violence, irresponsibility, and impulsive indiscretions. I treated a California highway patrol officer who had stolen a whiskey glass while on duty when he was drunk. He was fired from his job. His wife was so humiliated by his actions that she left him.

Note: Alcohol is any beverage or medication that contains any alcohol—from beer to wine to hard liquor, or even some cough syrups; drugs are any mind-altering substances that produce stimulant, depressant, or euphoric effects—amphetamines, barbiturates, marijuana, cocaine, heroin, PCP, and so on.

Go through the following list of symptoms of excessive alcohol or drug use and check off those that apply to you or your partner. This will give you an idea if this area is a problem.

1. Increasing consumption of alcohol or drugs, whether on a regular or sporadic basis, with frequent and perhaps unintended episodes of intoxication
2. Using drugs or alcohol as a means of handling problems
3. Obvious preoccupation with alcohol or drugs and the expressed need to have them
4. Gulping of drinks or using large quantities of drugs
5. The need for increasing quantities of alcohol or the drug to obtain the same "buzz"
6. Tendency toward making alibis and weak excuses for drinking or drug use
7. Needing to have others cover for you, either at work or at home
8. Refusal to concede what is obviously excessive consumption and expressing annoyance when the subject is mentioned
9. Frequent absenteeism from the job, especially if occurring in a pattern, such as following weekends and holidays (Monday morning "flu")
10. Repeated changes in jobs, particularly if to successively lower levels, or employment in a capacity beneath ability, education, and background
11. Shabby appearance, poor hygiene, and behavior and social adjustment inconsistent with previous levels or expectations
12. Persistent vague body complaints without apparent cause, particularly those of trouble sleeping, abdominal problems, headaches, or loss of appetite
13. Multiple contacts with the healthcare system
14. Persistent marital problems, perhaps multiple marriages
15. History of arrests for intoxicated driving or disorderly conduct
16. Unusual anxiety or obvious moodiness
17. Withdrawal symptoms on stopping (tremors, feeling extremely anxious, craving drugs or alcohol, vomiting, etc.); an alcoholic or drug abuser has usually tried to stop many times but was unable to withstand the symptoms of withdrawal

18. Hearing voices or seeing things that are not there
19. Blackouts (times you cannot remember)
20. Memory impairment
21. Drinking or using drugs alone; early morning use; secret use
22. Denial in the face of an obvious problem

My definition of an alcoholic or drug addict is anyone who has gotten into trouble (legal, relational, or work-related) while drinking or using drugs, yet who continues to use them. This person does not learn from negative experiences. A rational person would realize that he or she has trouble handling the alcohol or drugs and would stay away from them. The alcoholic or drug abuser denies that any problem exists and continues to use these substances. Unfortunately, many people with these problems have to experience repeated failures because of the substance use, and thus hit "rock bottom" before they seek treatment.

A helpful trend in medicine over the past ten years has been to classify alcoholism and drug abuse as illnesses instead of morally weak behavior. The American Medical Association, the World Health Organization, and many other professional groups regard these as specific disease entities. Untreated, these diseases progress to serious physical complications that often lead to death.

Here are some important facts you need to know about alcohol and drug abuse:

1. These addictions often run in families. The more relatives a person has who are alcoholics or addicts, the more likely the person is or will become dependent on chemicals. As a rule of thumb: one parent = 25% chance; two parents, or one parent and one sibling = 50% chance; three or more family members = 75%+ chance.

2. Alcoholism or drug addiction shortens life expectancy by an estimated ten to fifteen years.

3. Alcohol and drug addictions occur in about fifteen million Americans. If this problem applies to you, you are not alone.

4. There is no typical person with alcoholism or a drug addiction. These diseases affect people in all socio-economic classes.

5. Drunken driving or driving under the influence of drugs is responsible for well over 50 percent of the highway traffic fatalities.

6. Alcohol and drug addictions are treatable. Treatment for alcohol or drug abusers and their families is widely available today in all parts of the country.

Substance abuse often has a devastating impact on relationships. The associated feelings of shame, unpredictability, and loss of respect combine to undermine the foundation of a relationship. Good help is available for people who are afflicted with abuse problems and their families if they can get past the denial stage.

The Impact of Growing Up in an Alcohol- or Drug-Abusing Home: The pains of our childhood always haunt us, even if we have forgotten them, and even if it felt as though we were never a child.

Consider these facts:

- An estimated twenty-eight million Americans have at least one alcoholic parent.
- More than half of all alcoholics have an alcoholic parent.
- In up to 90 percent of child abuse cases, alcohol is a significant factor.
- Children of alcoholics are also frequently victims of incest, child neglect, and other forms of violence and exploitation.
- The majority of people served by employee assistance programs are adult children of alcoholics.
- Children of alcoholics are prone to experience a range of psychological difficulties, including learning disabilities, attention deficit disorders, anxiety, depression, attempted and completed suicides, eating disorders, and compulsive achieving.

Many people are kept from formulating and attaining their goals by their early emotional programming. For those who grew up in an alcoholic or drug-abusing family, the unpredictability and high level of emotional turmoil diverted their attention on a daily basis from their own healthy self-interests and filled their minds with obstacles that they face all of their lives.

A good deal of current medical literature, backed up by clinical experience, suggests that growing up in an alcoholic or drug-abusing environment has long-lasting and often devastating effects on how a person functions in the world, especially on their relationships. In my clinical practice, alcoholism and the effects of growing up in an alcoholic home are common problems. Past environment seriously affects self-esteem, the ability to parent, and the ability to love.

For those who grew up in an alcoholic or drug-abusing environment, consider the following generalizations and see if they apply to your life.

- Difficulty trusting others:
  The environment where one should learn trust was not trustworthy.
- Difficulty feeling strong emotions:
  Denial of feelings. Denial is one of the major hallmarks of an alcoholic home; "After all, we don't talk about such things."
- Difficulty expressing feelings:
  Will not talk. How could one talk about what happened at home? It was too embarrassing.

In essence, children who grow up in these homes:
- Don't trust
- Don't feel
- Don't talk

Researchers have found that the following characteristics are often seen in people who have grown up in alcoholic homes:

1. They guess at what normal behavior is.

2. They have difficulty following a project through from beginning to end.

3. They lie when it would be just as easy to tell the truth.

4. They judge themselves without mercy.

5. They have difficulty having fun.

6. They take themselves very seriously.

7. They have difficulty with intimate relationships.

8. They overreact to changes over which they have no control.

9. They constantly seek approval and affirmation.

10. They usually feel they are different from other people.

11. They are super-responsible or super-irresponsible.

12. They are extremely loyal even in the face of evidence that the loyalty is undeserved.

13. They are impulsive.

14. They feel like other people may be talking about them, which, growing up, may have been the case.

15. They have a sense of being inferior or damaged in some way.

16. They often feel that they are not important enough for others to want to talk to them.

17. They tend to marry alcoholics.

18. There is a much higher incidence of depression in women who grew up in an alcoholic home.

Recognizing these adult-children-of-alcoholic tendencies is the first step to changing the negative programming from the past. The impact of growing up in an alcoholic home often devastates relationships. A lack of trust, trouble talking, and difficulty feeling and expressing emotions impairs intimacy and often sets up an environment of suspicion and isolation. If you or your partner have ACA issues, get help to overcome these problems through a support group, reading books, or professional counseling. It can make the difference between a happy relationship and the end of a relationship.

ADULT ATTENTION DEFICIT DISORDER

Do you often feel restless? Have trouble concentrating? Have trouble with impulsiveness, either doing or saying things that you wish you hadn't? Do you fail to finish many projects you start? Are you easily bored or quick to anger? If the answer to most of these questions is yes, you might have the adult form of attention deficit disorder (ADD), what used to be called hyperactivity in children.

ADD is the most common psychiatric disorder in children, affecting 3–5 percent of children. Boys have a higher tendency to be hyperactive, girls with ADD tend to be spacey or daydreamers. In the 1980s, the name of this disorder was changed to attention deficit disorder because mental health professionals realized that there was more to this disorder than just hyperactivity. The main symptoms of ADD are a short attention span, easy distractibility, impulsiveness, and hyperactivity or restlessness. In fact, only about 50 percent of these children are hyperactive.

Until recently, most people thought that children outgrew this disorder in their teenage years. This is false. While it is true that the hyperactivity lessens over time, the other symptoms of impulsivity, distractibility, and a short attention span may remain into adulthood. Current research shows that 60–80 percent of these children never fully outgrow this disorder.

I treat many children with attention deficit disorder. When I meet with their parents and take a good family history, I find that there is about a 80 percent chance that at least one of the parents also had symptoms of ADD as a child and may, in fact, still show symptoms as an adult. Many of the parents were never diagnosed.

Often, I learn of ADD in adults when parents tell me that they have tried their child's medication and found it helpful. They report it helped them concentrate for longer periods of time, they became more organized, and were less impulsive.

Common symptoms of the adult form of ADD include: poor organization and planning, procrastination, trouble listening carefully to directions, and excessive traffic violations. Additionally, people with adult ADD are often late for appointments, frequently misplace things, may be quick to anger and have poor follow-through. They may also change jobs frequently and may manage their finances poorly. Substance abuse, especially alcohol or amphetamines and cocaine, and low self-esteem are also common.

Many people do not recognize the seriousness of this disorder in children and just pass these kids off as defiant and willful. Yet, ADD is a serious disorder. If left untreated, it affects a child's self-esteem, social relationships, and ability to learn. Several studies have shown that up to 40 percent of these children are arrested for a felony by the time they are sixteen. Also, 30 percent never finish high school; 75 percent have interpersonal problems as adults, and 30 percent have problems with drug or alcohol abuse.

Many adults with ADD tell me that when they were children they were in trouble all the time. They had a genuine sense of being different. Even though many of the adults I treat with ADD are bright, they are frequently frustrated by not living up to their potential.

According to Russell Barkley, Ph.D. of the University of Massachusetts, a diagnosis of adult ADD requires that a person have at least three of the following twelve symptoms (five or six symptoms make this disorder very likely). These symptoms must not be part of another psychiatric disorder, such as substance abuse or depression, and they must have been present since childhood.

- trouble sustaining attention
- difficulty completing projects
- easily overwhelmed by tasks of daily living
- trouble maintaining an organized work/living area
- inconsistent work performance
- lacks attention to detail

- makes decisions impulsively
- difficulty delaying gratification, stimulation seeking
- restless, fidgety
- makes comments without considering their impact
- impatient, easily frustrated
- frequent traffic violations

Recently, it has become clear that ADD is a neurological disorder with a biological basis. Metabolic brain studies reveal that when a person with ADD tries to concentrate, the front part of the brain, which controls concentration levels, goes slower rather than faster. In a sense, their brain deactivates when the person tries to use it. Stimulant medication is the treatment of choice for this disorder, since the problem exists because the brain is understimulated.

For children, teens, or adults, ADD often negatively affects their ability to interact with others. Here are some of the reasons:

Social isolation—Many people with ADD have failed in relationships so much in the past that they do not want to experience this pain anymore. Their outrageous behavior also often ostracizes them from their peer group.

Fighting—Fighting is typical for many people with ADD. It may be related to impulsivity (saying things without thinking), seeking stimulating behavior, misperceptions, rage outbursts, and chronically low self-esteem.

Misperceptions—This often causes serious problems in relationships. Often the spouse of an ADD person has to spend an inordinate amount of time correcting misperceptions that lead to disagreements. On the night before he was leaving on a business trip, a man told his wife, who had ADD, that he was going to miss her. She heard him say, "I'm not going to miss you," and she was angry with him for the rest of the night.

Distractibility—Due to distractibility, conversations

are often cut short or left incomplete, leaving the other person feeling unimportant.

Problems taking turns—The ADD person's need to have what they want right away often causes problems in situations where they need to take turns, such as in conversations or games.

Speaking without thinking—This is perhaps the most damaging result of ADD to relationships. Just because a person has a thought doesn't mean that it is accurate or that they necessarily must believe it. Many people with ADD just say what comes to mind. They then get stuck defending such statements, which causes further problems.

Problems completing chores—This leads to many resentments.

Sensitivity to noise—When the ADD person is sensitive to noise, they often need to escape from others to feel calm or peaceful inside.

Sensitivity to touch—When the person is sensitive to touch, they often shy away from affection. This can harm a relationship, especially if the person's partner wants or needs affection.

Excessive talking—Sometimes people with ADD talk, just to talk, and end up not saying much. This irritates others because if they don't listen, the ADD person becomes upset.

Lack of talking—The partners of other ADD people complain that there is little talking in the relationship. "He seems turned off when he comes home," is a common complaint.

Disorganization—This causes problems in a relationship because the ADD person often doesn't live up to their part of the chores or agreements.

Takes high risks/thrill-seeking—This type of behavior worries the parents, partners, or friends of the ADD person. Friends often feel pressured to go along with dangerous behavior, causing a rift in the relationship.

Easily frustrated/emotional/moody—Many family members of ADD children, teens, and adults have told me that they never know what to expect from the ADD person. "One minute she's happy, the next minute she's screaming," is a common complaint. Small amounts of stress may trigger huge explosions.

Tantrums/rage outbursts—Some studies indicate that up to 85 percent of people with ADD have rage outbursts, often with little provocation. After this occurs several times in a relationship, the parent, partner, or friend becomes "gun shy" and starts to withdraw from the person. Untreated ADD is often involved in abusive relationships.

Low self-esteem—When people do not feel good about themselves, it impairs their ability to relate to others. They have difficulty taking compliments or getting outside of themselves to truly understand another person. The brain filters information from the environment. When the brain's filter (self-esteem) is negative, people tend to see just the negative and ignore any positive. Many partners of ADD people complain that when they compliment their partners, they find a way to make it look as if they have just been criticized.

Looking for turmoil—This is a common complaint of people living with someone who has ADD. They say that the person looks for trouble. Rather than ignoring a minor incident, he or she focuses on it and has difficulty letting it go. Things in an ADD house do not remain peaceful for long.

Chronic anxiety or restlessness—As already mentioned, ADD people often feel restless or anxious. This often causes them to search for ways to relax. They may use excessive sex, food, or alcohol to try to calm themselves. I treated one man who had had sex with his girlfriend more than five hundred times in the last year of their relationship. She left him, because she felt that their relationship was only based upon sex.

Failure to see others' needs—Many people with ADD have trouble getting outside of themselves to see the emotional needs of others. They are often labeled as spoiled, immature, or self-centered.

Lack of learning from the past—Often people with

ADD engage in repetitive, negative arguments with others. They do not seem to learn from the interpersonal mistakes from their past, and they repeat them again and again.

Chronic procrastination—The ADD person often waits until the last minute to do things (pay bills, buy birthday, anniversary, or Christmas gifts, etc.). This irritates those around them.

If you think that you or someone you love has adult ADD, it is important to have a thorough evaluation by a psychiatrist, and if possible by a child psychiatrist since they have the most experience with this disorder. Many adult psychiatrists and family physicians have little experience with adult ADD.

There are usually three components to treating adult ADD. The first component involves medication. Many adults respond to the same stimulants, such as Ritalin and Dexedrine, that are prescribed for children. For those who don't respond or who have high levels of anxiety or depression, we often use an antidepressant, such as Norpramin or Prozac. But as with children, medication alone is never adequate treatment. Therefore, the second component includes relationship counseling and anger management, and the third component involves time management and problem-solving skills.

With good care ADD is a highly treatable disorder in children or adults. Without treatment, there are potentially serious consequences in a person's ability to work and to love. I believe this disorder is the underlying reason for a great many people sabotaging their lives.

PREMENSTRUAL TENSION SYNDROME

"One week she loves me and can't keep her hands off me. The next two weeks she doesn't seem to care one way or the other. The fourth week, everything I do is wrong and I just try to stay out of her way." These were words recently told to me by the husband of a woman with premenstrual tension syndrome

(PMS). Between 20 and 30 percent of women are afflicted with symptoms of PMS. For some women, the problems are mild and include bloating, breast tenderness, moodiness, and irritability. Some women have moderately more intense symptoms where they have considerably more negativity. Other women have an extreme form of PMS associated with severe depression, anger, rage, and in some cases violence.

Sherry was a thirty-five-year-old nurse who had severe cyclic mood changes, starting ten days before the onset of her menstrual cycle. On three separate occasions during this period of her cycle, she left her husband. On the last occasion she attacked him with a knife. During the good times of her cycle (the first twenty days), her husband reported that they got along well. "But when she gets that look in her eyes and that tone in her voice," he said, "I know to stay away from her." I first met Sherry during the part of her cycle when she felt the best. She was a petite woman who seemed soft-spoken and easy-going. It was hard to believe that she could attack anyone with a knife. Because of the drastic mood changes, I decided to study the function of her brain.

She had a nuclear medicine brain study that evaluated blood flow and metabolism four days before the onset of her menstrual flow (at her worst time) and again seven days after the onset of her menstrual flow (during her best time). The results were fascinating! Four days before the onset of her period, at her worst time, her limbic system, which is the part of the brain that controls emotions, was markedly overactive, especially on the left side. When the limbic system is overactive, I have found that people have problems with depression and negativity. When the left side is more active than the right side they often have a problem with a short fuse and violence. When Sherry's brain function was studied eleven days later, during her best time, her limbic system was normal. With the brain study findings and the cyclic nature of her severe mood swings, I decided to try her on a medication called valproic acid that we use on people with severe mood swings. Within several days, she reported that overall she was sleeping better, not grinding her teeth, and she felt more relaxed. Through the subsequent nine menstrual cycles, she did not go through the cyclic mood changes.

Even though most PMS problems are not as severe as Sherry's, PMS has devastated many relationships. Some husbands have told me that they keep a monthly log on their wives to know when to plan business or fishing trips away from home. Currently, there is no standard treatment for PMS. Some of the ones my patients found helpful include:

- high daily doses of Vitamin B6 (300–400 milligrams)
- exercise
- eliminating foods high in simple sugars, such as candy, cake, or ice cream.
- hormonal therapies with birth control pills
- medications such as Prozac or valproic acid.

If you notice that PMS is a problem in your life, it is important that you seek the answer best suited to you. Your relationship might depend on it.

WHEN TWO PEOPLE IN A RELATIONSHIP HAVE EMOTIONAL PROBLEMS

Given the high number of people who will suffer from emotional problems (48 percent), it is not surprising to see couples where both partners have emotional difficulties. This can make the relationship extremely challenging.

Janice and Harry were referred to me by their marriage counselor who was ready to give up on them. "I tried everything I could think of," she told me. "Nothing works." The counselor told me that Janice would tearfully talk about the same problems over and over and that Harry never seemed to listen. They were caught in a vicious cycle. When I first met with this couple, the hostility pervaded the atmosphere. They sat at opposite ends of the couch and never made eye contact. They told me that I was their last stop before the attorney's office. As I took a detailed history, it was clear that Janice had symptoms of an obsessive-compulsive disorder. I learned that she checked the stove and house locks four times before going to bed and she was upset when things were out of place. She tended to lock onto thoughts; she was an incessant worrier; and she held tightly onto past hurts. Harry, on the other hand, had clear symptoms of attention deficit disorder. He was restless and fidgety. He had a short attention span and was easily distracted. He was terribly disorganized, easily frustrated, and chronically late. He did not have the patience to listen to Janice go on and on. He was also impulsive and he would blurt out hurtful statements. "They would just come out. As soon as they left my mouth, I knew I'd pay for them for weeks or months because of how she holds things," Harry told me. Harry did poorly in school, despite his intelligence. He had behavioral problems and his mother described him as hyperactive.

Given that I was this couple's last stop, I decided that we had no time to waste. I started Janice on Prozac (an antiobsessive and antidepressant medication) and Harry on Ritalin (a stimulant used to treat ADD). At our follow-up appointment, I knew something was different. Janice and Harry sat next to each other. She had her hand on his leg, and he paid close attention to what she said. Janice did not go on and on, but said things one time, and she expressed a desire to let go of the hurts from the past. Both noticed the positive changes in each other, and they felt able to improve their relationship. Two years later, this couple was together, loving and supportive of each other. They were able to get outside of themselves and see each other's needs. Some people might argue that their relationship was artificially repaired by medication, but it was their underlying emotional disorders that had hindered the success of their relationship.

Recognize problems and get help when necessary. It may make the difference between a happy relationship and no relationship at all.

WHY MEN HAVE TROUBLE SEEKING HELP

When Janice and Harry first started to have marital problems, Janice wanted to get help but Harry refused. He said that he didn't want to air his problems in front of a stranger. It wasn't until Janice threatened to leave him that he finally agreed to go to counseling.

Initially, Harry listed many reasons why he wouldn't go for help: he didn't see that the problems were that bad; it was too much money; he thought all counselors were "messed up," and he didn't want to be perceived as crazy by anyone who might find out about the counseling.

Unfortunately, Harry's attitude is common among men. Many men, when faced with obvious problems in their marriages, their children, or even themselves, refuse to see problems. Their lack of awareness and strong tendency toward denial prevent them from seeking help until more damage has been done than necessary. In Harry's case, he had to be threatened with divorce before he would go.

Some people may say it is unfair for me to pick on men. And indeed, some men see problems long before some women. Overall, however, mothers see problems in children before fathers and are more willing to seek help, and many more wives call for marital counseling than husbands. What is it in our society that causes men to overlook obvious problems, to deny problems until it is too late to deal with them effectively or until more damage was done than necessary? Some of the answers may be found in how boys are raised in our society, the societal expectations we place on men, and the overwhelming pace of many men's daily lives.

Boys most often engage in active play (sports, war games, video games, etc.) that involves little dialogue or communication. The games often involve dominance and submissiveness, winning and losing, and little interpersonal communication; rather, problems are handled by force, strength, or skill. Girls, on the other hand, often engage in more interpersonal or communicative types of play, such as dolls and storytelling. When my wife was little, she used to line up her dolls to teach them. Fathers often take their sons out to throw the ball around or shoot hoops rather than to go for a walk and talk.

Many men retain the childhood notions of competition and that one must be better than others to be any good at all. To admit to a problem is to be less than other men. As a result, many men wait to seek help until their problem is obvious to the whole world. Other men feel totally responsible for all that happens in their families and admitting to a problem is to admit that they have in some way failed.

Clearly, the pace of life prevents some men from being able to take the time to look clearly at the important people in their lives and their relationships with them. When I spend time with fathers and husbands and help them slow down enough to see what is really important to them, more often than not they begin to see the problems and work toward more helpful solutions. The issue is not one of being uncaring or uninterested, it is seeing what is there.

Chapter 7

Two Minutes to Total Focus: Overview

The Two-Minute Focus Statement is what you will use to keep yourself on track in your relationship every day. It is a written synthesis of your hopes, dreams, and goals. By looking at this statement daily (which will take about two minutes) you will stay *totally focused* on what you want in the relationship. *Total focus* is essential to reaching any goal. In the next six chapters we will develop the framework for your Two-Minute Focus Statement. We will do this by exploring in detail each of the areas covered in the Two-Minute Focus Statement and then have you develop a specific focus statement for each area. We will look at:

1. Relationship issues: Your attitudes and assumptions toward each other, your communication patterns, your time together, your child-rearing practices, and problem-solving skills.

2. Sexuality issues: Emotional bonding, sexual and nonsexual touching, helpful sexual thoughts, emotional and physical stimulation, compatibility, your desires, your partner's desires, the best environment for physical love, turn-offs, and turn-ons.

3. Fun: The necessity of fun in a relationship, how much time you devote to fun, fun together and separately, and doing things you have never done before.

4. Work issues both inside and outside of the home: How work can bring a couple together, unconscious work programming, work values, the goals of work, being work's master and not its slave, rules to master work, and work mechanics.

5. Money issues: Who handles the money, how it is handled, emotional issues and money, practical issues and money, being on the same playing field in regards to money, and financial goals.

6. Personal issues: Meaning and purpose, intellectual growth, spiritual health, emotional health, and physical health.

As you go through each section, pick out the areas that are most important to you. Keep notes as you go along to ensure the ideas and concepts that are special to you end up in your final Two-Minute Focus Statement. At the end of each chapter you will develop a clear focus statement that will then be incorporated into your completed Two-Minute Focus Statement in Chapter Thirteen. I will give you a sample Two-Minute Focus Statement from my own life. Take this assignment seriously. It will have an impact on the rest of your life if you allow it to.

Chapter 8
Shared Relationship Focus
Attitudes and assumptions, communication, time, raising children, handling conflict/problem-solving

- What is your attitude toward your partner?
- How do you think about the relationship?
- Do you perceive your relationship as a positive force in your life or is it a drain on your energy?
- Do you find time to be together, or do you end up with the crumbs of the day?
- How is the communication between you and your partner?
- Do you understand each other, or does it seem that you are always trying to clarify what you mean?
- Is physical affection an area in your relationship that brings you closer, or is it an area of contention?
- Do you know your partner's innermost dreams and desires, or are you frustrated because your dreams and desires go unmet?
- If you have children, how good are you at shared parenting?
- Do you support each other, or are you at odds with each other?
- Does your relationship fall apart when there are problems, or have you developed problem-solving skills that help you weather the difficult times?

Many couples never ask themselves these critical questions. You are different. Just the act of asking yourself these questions can change your relationship forever. This chapter will help you focus on how you want to interact with or relate to your partner around the issues of attitude and perceptions, time, communication, child-rearing, and problem-solving. Developing clear goals for each of these areas will direct your behavior to be much more effective day-to-day.

ATTITUDE AND PERCEPTION

Attitude is everything. It is the way we, as individuals, perceive and approach the world around us. Our five senses take in the world, but our attitude filters all incoming information. When our attitude is good, we process information positively. When our attitude is angry or hostile, we perceive the world negatively. Our attitude toward the outside world is based on our inside world. For example, when we feel stressed we are much more likely to be irritated by behavior that usually doesn't bother us. When we feel depressed, we tend to filter almost everything through negativity. On the other hand, when we feel positive and happy, we tend to overlook or be more understanding when someone else is having a bad day. Our attitudes bear witness to our state of mind.

To be healthy in a relationship, you have to be responsible for your own attitude. It is important to understand that no one can make you do or feel anything. Your underlying thoughts and perceptions control your behavior. Believing this important point is the only way you can gain control over your actions and feelings. If you do not believe this principle, you will tend to blame your partner for your bad feelings or for your negative actions. You will become a victim of your behavior. Victim mentality in a relationship is extremely harmful because it renders you powerless to change your life.

Perception

It is how you perceive situations, rather than the actual situations themselves, that causes you to do what you do. Memorize the "perception equation":

$A + B = C$

A is the actual event, B is how we interpret or perceive the event, and C is how we react to the event.

Other people or events (A) can't cause us to do anything. It is our interpretation or perception (B) that causes our behavior and our feelings (C). For example, a wife yawned during a conversation with her husband. He accused her of being bored with him and stormed off. Later when they talked about the event, she said that she wasn't bored, just tired. She was under pressure at work and had not slept the previous night. Her yawning was the event or A; his interpretation that she was bored was B; and his storming off was how he reacted, or C. I taught this couple to confirm the truth of their assumptions with each other rather than resort to mind-reading. The B stuff, as I refer to how we perceive or interpret situations, determines how we react to others, not the A stuff. In the above example, the husband's interpretation of his wife's behavior was automatically negative. If he had challenged his initial negative perception, he could have avoided storming off.

Attitudes and perceptions (the B stuff) between a couple are based on several important factors, including:

- childhood programming
- history in the relationship
- current health and stress hormone levels

Childhood Programming

Childhood programming plays a significant role in how we perceive interactions with others. If you were constantly disappointed by one of your parents, then it is likely you will expect to be disappointed by other important people in your life. If your parents controlled you with anger, then any anger on the part of your spouse is likely to set off negative feelings within you.

To understand your own programming in relationships, it is often helpful to write an autobiography. The autobiography doesn't have to be long, but must include several important ingredients. Start with writing what you know, good and bad, about your grandparents on both sides. (Often patterns are passed down for three or four generations.) Next, write down significant memories about your parents, the good stuff and the bad stuff. Then, starting from birth, from pictures and what others have told you, write something, good and bad, for each year of your life. Also, write about times when you experienced the following emotions: sadness, anger, anxiety, despair, joy, contentment, excitement, and hope. If you put effort into developing this personal profile, many significant patterns will begin to emerge. Some people begin to see early patterns of self-doubt or self-hatred, which now they can begin to question. Many patients have said to me, "I never liked myself as a kid, but I was just a kid. What could I have done that was so terrible?" Writing about your own life will often give you clues into why you do the things you do. It will help you understand your attitudes and actions in your relationships.

History in a Relationship

History in a relationship also plays an important role in your current attitude. When you have a history of love, care, and concern, your attitude will likely be positive. When you have a history of anger, betrayal, or dishonesty, your attitude will likely be negative. This is one reason why it is so important to be thoughtful in a relationship. Without a history of kindness and caring in a relationship, it is hard to weather the inevitable stormy times that all relationships face. Seek to build a solid history together.

Current Health and Stress Levels

Current health and stress levels also play an important role in your attitudes toward and assumptions about each other. When you are feeling sick or stressed, it is important to take care of your relationships. You need them for support. Yet, many people take out their pain or frustration on their partners when they are not feeling well. One of my patients became depressed after his mother died suddenly. Initially, his wife and children were supportive. They allowed him the time and space to vent his sadness, and they were available to talk with him whenever he needed to talk. Like most men, however, he didn't talk much about his sadness. After several months, his sadness over his mother's death turned to rage. He frequently yelled at the children, belittled his wife in front of the children, and blamed his wife and the children for his bad feelings. It got to the point where no one wanted to be around him, and they avoided him as much as possible. Initially, he refused to get counseling for himself, blaming everyone else for the problems in the family. Finally, after his work was affected, he sought help. Dealing with his sadness and grief helped him to dump most of his anger, and he could reconnect with his own loved ones. Too often our own stress levels cause us to assume negative things about those around us.

In any successful relationship, it is critical to have a baseline attitude of care and respect, and then to filter information about the other person through that attitude. I referred to this concept in Chapter Three as PBAs, or positive basic assumptions, about the other person. Just believing that your partner cares about you cuts down on the number of problems in relationships. When you get caught in expecting the worst from another person, you often unconsciously set it up to get just what you expect. Now if you have concrete evidence that the other person wants to hurt you, that's a different story. These positive basic assumptions are critical to the success of most relationships.

Make it your goal to assume the best about your partner and to set up an encouraging, supportive, and positive atmosphere in the relationship.

Attitude Questions
- What is your current attitude toward your partner?
- What do you believe their attitude is toward you?
- What are the programmed messages you received from your parents about intimate relationships?
- What are the programmed messages you believe your partner received from his or her parents about intimate relationships?
- What type of attitude do you want to have toward your partner?
- What type of attitude do you want your partner to have toward you?

TIME

A concept that often is lost in relationships is time—actual, physical time together. In the accelerated pace of life, time together is often the first casualty of the relationship. Yet, time together is essential for a healthy relationship. Not time at the end of the day when you are both dead tired, but the best time of the week. Many people give their best hours to their jobs and starve their relationships.

When people start out in a relationship, they can't wait to spend time with each other. They look for ways to be together. They do fun things, such as dinners, concerts, plays, movies, and athletic activities. They long to be together. As they become more comfortable in the relationship other things take precedence, and the time together diminishes.

After a while some couples claim that they do not have common interests, they do not like doing the same things together. This can become a big problem if a couple does not learn to handle it. Several years ago two friends of mine came to me for help. I had known Jonathan and Sharon most of my life and had always wondered why they got married. They were so different. Jonathan loved to hunt and fish, Sharon loved to shop and do crafts. Every time Jonathan had a break from work he would go hunting or fishing with his friends. Sharon spent her free time shopping with friends or doing craft work. They even had a marked difference in the types of movies they liked. Jonathan loved action movies (which were too violent for Sharon), and Sharon liked romantic movies (which were too mushy for Jonathan). Whenever Jonathan planned his trips, Sharon complained that she wanted more time with him. Jonathan's standard answer was that they were different, and they liked to do different things. Sharon grew more resentful when they had children and she was left at home to care for them while Jonathan was off on his trips. The trouble escalated when one of the children was hospitalized while Jonathan was on a trip, and she could not reach him. Sharon was tired of their differences and wanted more time together or wanted to "trade him in." Jonathan got the message. He wanted things to work out at home, he didn't want to be "traded in," but he was too busy focusing on other things to notice Sharon's unhappiness. They agreed to compromise. One week Sharon would choose what they would do together, the next week it was Jonathan's turn. To their surprise, they both enjoyed learning new things. Sharon had fun fishing and learning to shoot. Jonathan found he liked tole painting, he had never been exposed to it before. Although he still had trouble with mushy movies, he went with Sharon because he realized his goal was not to just do what he wanted to do, his goal was to have a wonderful relationship with his wife. Time together is essential for healthy relationships.

To protect your relationship from the erosions of everyday living, it is critical to protect your time together. Many people will try to take your time, but it is critical to prioritize the time you have. There is a lengthy discussion on how to spend time together in the chapter on fun. For now, I want you to commit some time to your relationship every day and some of the best times of your week to each other.

Time, like money, is a valuable commodity if you

spend it wisely. But, also like money, if you overcommit yourself you will discover that you are always stressed by all the commitments you make. Spend your time in a way that matches your goals for your life!

Time Questions

- How much individual time do you have alone with your partner?
- What is the quality of your time together (fun, relaxed, tense, or cool)?
- What do you do when you are alone together?
- What would you like to do?
- How is your ability to compromise and alternate what you do together?

COMMUNICATION

Poor communication is at the center of many relational problems. Jumping to conclusions, mind-reading, and "having to be right" are only a few traits that doom communication. When people do not connect with each other meaningfully, the relationship becomes only what it is in their separate minds, and many imaginary problems arise.

I treated one patient who was frequently angry at her husband. During the day, she often imagined their evening together; they would spend time talking and her husband would be attentive to her needs. When he actually came home tired and frustrated from a hard day at work, he ignored her. She felt disappointed and reacted angrily toward him. Her husband often was bewildered about what was wrong. He was unaware of his wife's thoughts during the day and didn't know why he was disappointing her. After six sessions with this couple, the wife learned how to express her needs openly and she discovered a receptive husband.

Too often in relationships we have expectations and hopes that we never clearly communicate to our partners. We assume they should know what we need, and we are disappointed when they don't read our minds accurately. Clear communication is essential if relationships are to be mutually satisfying.

Here are fourteen ways that communication can be sabotaged in relationships. Avoid these when possible.

- Poor attitude. This is where, for example, you expect the conversation to go nowhere, so you don't even try.
- Negative assumptions about the other person. Up front you don't trust the other person, and you remain stiff and guarded during your time together.
- Unclear expectations and needs. This is when you expect the other person to guess what you want or need. It is great when others can anticipate our needs, but most people are so busy that it is hard for them to see the needs of other people. That does not make them good or bad. It means it is important to tell people what you need.
- No reinforcing body language. Body language is so important because it sends conscious and unconscious messages. When two people are having a discussion, and one person fails to make eye contact or acknowledge the other person with facial or body gestures, the person who is talking begins to feel lost, alone, and unenthusiastic about continuing the conversation. Eye contact and physical acknowledgement are essential to good communication.
- Competing with distractions. Distractions frequently doom communication. It is not a good idea, for example, for my wife to talk to me about something important during the fourth quarter of a playoff game. Likewise, if I need to talk with her, it is best done during commercials when her favorite show is on. Decrease distractions to have clear communication. Also, being unable to hear, either because you are too far away from the other person, or the other person is talking too softly, can be an easily corrected problem.

- Never asking for feedback on what you are saying. Many people assume that they are sending clear messages to the other person, who actually understands something completely different from what was meant. Feedback is essential to clear communication.
- Kitchen-sinking. This occurs in arguments when one person feels backed into a corner, and he or she brings up unrelated issues from the past to protect him- or herself or to intensify the disagreement. Stay on task until you discuss an issue fully.
- Mind-reading. This is where you arbitrarily predict what another person is thinking and then react to that imagined information. Mind-reading is often a projection of what the "mind-reader" him- or herself is thinking. Even after couples have been married for thirty years, it is impossible for them always to be right about what is going on in the other person's head.
- Faking attention. Pretending to listen when you are really thinking about something else.
- Having to be right. This destroys effective communication. When a person has to be right in a conversation, there is no communication, only debate.
- Sparring. Using put-downs, sarcasm, or discounting the other's ideas erodes meaningful dialogue and creates distance in relationships.
- Starting to think about your own responses before you've fully heard what the speaker wishes to say. Many people actually turn off shortly after a speaker begins, remembering only the point they wish to make themselves. Keep an open mind.
- Persistence. Often it takes repeated efforts to get what you need. It is important not to give up. When people give up asking for what they need, they often silently resent the other person, which subverts the whole relationship. Persistence is important to getting what you want.

- Not understanding the natural differences between men and women. Men and women communicate differently. In general, men are briefer in their communication, to the point, less emotional, and more in a "problem-solving mode." Men are often more competitive during communication than women. In general, women want more communication, communicate for longer periods of time, are less direct, and more emotional. They are often in a communication and interpersonal connection mode rather than the problem-solving mode. Women are less competitive during communication, although, according to some communication experts, this seems to have changed over the past twenty years. Understanding these differences can help couples stay on the same communication wavelengths or at least recognize when they are not, and see it as a gender issue rather than a good or bad issue.

Here are four exercises to help you communicate more effectively with your partner.

I. The Echo Technique

The "I hear you saying" or echo technique, is a start toward truly understanding your partner by first understanding what he or she is saying. This technique involves repeating back what you understand has been said before you respond. In this way, you check out with the sender whether the message you received is the one they intended to send. Communication often breaks down because of distortions between intention and understanding, especially in emotionally charged encounters. Simply saying, "I hear you saying... Is that what you meant?" can help avoid misunderstandings. This technique is particularly helpful when you suspect a breakdown in communication.

Different phrases to use in this technique could include:

- "I heard you say... Am I right?"
- "Did you mean to say...?"
- "I'm not sure I understand what you said. Did you say...?"
- "Did I understand you correctly? Are you saying that...?"
- "Let me see if I understand what you're saying to me. You said that...?"

Advantages to this "I hear you saying" technique include:
- You receive more accurate messages.
- Misunderstandings are cleared up immediately.
- You are forced to give your full attention to the other person.
- Both parties are now responsible for accurate communication.
- The sender is likely to be more careful with what he/she says.
- It increases your ability to really hear the other person and thus learn from him/her.
- It prevents you from thinking about what you are going to say next, and instead allows you to hear what the other person is saying.
- It increases communication.
- It tends to cool down conflicts.

Practice this technique at least twice this week. See if it doesn't increase your communication abilities and thus your understanding of your partner.

II. Mirroring
Your ability to understand and communicate with others will be enhanced by learning what psychiatrists call the mirroring technique. You can use this technique in any interpersonal situation to increase rapport with those around you.

When you mirror someone, you assume or imitate his body language—posture, eye contact, and facial expression—and you use the same words and phrases in conversation that the other person uses. For example, if someone is leaning forward in his chair, looking intensely at you, you, without making it obvious, do the same. If you note that he uses the same phrase several times, such as, "I believe we have a winner here," pick it up and make it part of your vocabulary for that conversation.

This is not mimicry, which implies ridicule; rather, this technique helps the other person establish an unconscious identification with you in his or her mind. Attempt to use this mirroring technique at least once a day for a week.

III. Get-Outside-of-Yourself Exercise

The echoing and mirroring techniques will help you out with this exercise. The next couple of times you disagree with someone, take their side of the argument. At least verbally, begin to agree with their point of view. Argue for it, understand it, see where they are coming from. Although this can be a difficult exercise, it will pay royally if you use it to learn to understand others better.

Note: To do this exercise effectively, you must first listen to the opposing point of view without interrupting. True listening is difficult, but if you concentrate on echoing back what you heard, you will be almost there.

IV. What-to-Do-When-You-Are-Dumped-on-This-Week Exercise

Taking your partner's assaults too personally is often a mistake. Often, when your partner is "reading you the riot act," he or she is doing it because he or she had a bad day, and it may have nothing to do with you. One thing that will help you in such situations is to realize this fact: When someone dumps on you, it may have *nothing to do with you* and everything to do with him or her.

The next time your partner unloads on you, ask yourself two questions:

- What may be going on with your partner that is causing him or her to act that way?
- Did you do something to contribute to the situation?

If you did something, try to correct it. If not, try not to take the situation too personally. If possible, don't make other people's problems your problems.

Clear communication is essential to a healthy relationship.

Communication Questions
- How did/do your parents communicate with each other?
- How did/do your partner's parents communicate with each other?
- How is your communication with your partner?
- Of the traps discussed in this chapter, which ones do you fall into?
- Which of the communication techniques can you put to use right now?

RAISING CHILDREN

Few experiences are more gratifying in a marriage than raising children. Also, few experiences are as stressful or as frustrating in a marriage as raising children. Child rearing brings up so many different emotional issues between a couple that it is essential for them to have clearly defined goals for what they want for themselves as parents and what they want for their children. Parenting is best done together, with common goals.

Clearly stated, common goals take parenting behavior out of the realm of the unconscious and place it in the present. Many parents relive with their children what was done to them as children. It is what they were programmed to do. Other parents do the opposite of what their parents did, still rebelling against what happened to them. Both postures may be harmful to children. It is critical to know what you want for yourself as a parent and to know what you want for your child. With focused goals you are more likely to match your behavior to get what you want.

Here is a set of parenting goals that I use to focus my behavior with my children. Add your own special touches to them, and put them up where you can see these goals every day. Then ask yourself, "Is my behavior getting me what I want as a parent and what I want for my child?"

As a parent—**The overall goal is to be competent and to be a positive force in the child's life.**

1. Be involved—I want to be there for my children, so I will ensure that I have enough time for them. When I was growing up my father worked all the time. Literally, all the time. He owns a chain of grocery stores in southern California, and to build his business, he worked from before I was up in the morning to after I went to bed at night. The only time I saw him was when he took me to work with him. As a child I was not happy about his frequent absences. I wanted him to go to my little league games, read me stories, and spend time with me. He grew up in the depression, and he was programmed to work to overcome hardship. As a teenager, I remember thinking that I would spend more time with my children than my father did with me. But as a father I found myself working a great deal of the time. My unconscious programming was that men work all the time. Having the goal of being involved helps me focus on what I truly want and what is good for me and my children.

2. Be open—I will talk with them in a manner that makes it easier for them to talk to me when they need to. Openness and receptiveness to children is essential to a good relationship with them. I teach parents that almost any form of discipline will work if you have a good relationship with your children and that almost any form of discipline won't work if you have a bad relationship with them. Be open, be a good listener, and let them know you are interested in their thoughts.

3. Be firm/set limits—I will provide appropriate supervision and limits until my children develop their own moral/internal controls. Many parents who grew up in the sixties have lost the concept of authority. In fact, they still harbor the notion that authority is a bad word. These parents grew up during the Vietnam War when people demonstrated against authority. They have trouble accepting that their children should respect them. They are also unsure that being firm is good for children. Solid research shows that being firm with children is essential to their well-being. Parents who have trouble setting limits for their children emotionally handicap them. Children need clear expectations, limits, and boundaries; otherwise, they never learn to respect other children, and they have difficulty with authority figures, such as teachers or coaches. Limits are essential to ensure the emotional health of children (and their parents).

4. Be together—Whether parents are married or divorced, it is best for children when the parents agree and support each other. Children are often experts at creating rifts between their parents. It is one of the ways they gain power and control in a family. Short-circuit their games by supporting each other, checking with each other, and keeping your disagreements about them in private.

5. Be kind—I will raise my children in a way that ensures they will want to come see me after they leave home. Being a parent is also a selfish job. Kindness is essential to teaching children about life. When you are kind to children, you enhance your bond with them, and they want to become more like you. When you are mean or cruel to children, you strain the bond with them, and they are likely to choose values that oppose yours.

6. Be fun—I will joke, clown, and play with my kids. Having fun is essential to both physical and emotional health. Children learn the concept of fun from their parents. If you are always serious, odds are they will grow up to be serious. If you play, joke, and kid with them, they are more likely to be able to do those things with their children. Teach them how to play and have fun by playing with them.

For children—**The overall goal is to enhance development.**

1. Be relational—We live in a relational world. It is imperative that I teach my children how to get along with others. Children are not born knowing the ropes. You need to teach them about relationships. It is important to teach them about sharing and give-and-take. It is essential that you give them the opportunities to interact with other children and to establish a time when you discuss with them their friendships and relationship frustrations.

2. Be responsible—My children need to believe and act as if they have some control over their own lives, that what happens to them is not always someone else's fault. Otherwise, they act like victims. Don't allow children to blame everyone else for their problems. Teach them to have a sense of control over their lives; teach them that their actions can make a positive difference. Too many parents allow children to blame the lousy teacher or the mean child for the problems they have, and they never encourage the child to look at the part he or she played in a situation gone wrong. If you help your children take responsibility early in their lives, they are much more likely to be successful in their adulthood.

3. Be independent—I will allow my children to have some choices over their own lives so that they will be able to make good decisions on their own. For children to learn independence, they need to be able to make some of the decisions in their lives. With your supervision it is important for them to have some say over the clothes they wear, how they wear their hair, and what interests they pursue. When parents make all the decisions for a child it breeds dependence and low self-esteem.

4. Be self-confident—I will encourage my children to be involved in various activities that will help them build a sense of competence. Self-confidence often comes from our ability to be able to master tasks and sports. Provide the opportunities and training for them to become competent in areas of their interest.

5. Be self-accepting—I will notice more positive traits than negative ones in my children to teach them to be able to accept themselves. You program a child's attitude toward him- or herself by what you notice about them. If you spend time with them, they will believe they are important. If you notice more good than bad in them, they will notice more good than bad in themselves.

6. Be adaptable—I will expose my children to different situations so that they will be flexible enough to deal with the various stresses that will come their way. Don't do for children the things they can do for themselves. Teaching children to be competent and adaptable is one of the greatest gifts you can give them.

7. Be emotionally free—I will allow my children the ability to express themselves in an accepting environment. I will also seek help for my children if they show prolonged symptoms of emotional trouble. Despite the best efforts of parents, some children have emotional problems. Teach them to obtain help when they have a problem by not ignoring their problems when they are young.

8. Be fun—I will teach my child how to have fun and how to laugh. Teaching children to play, have fun, and feel good is essential to their emotional health.

Share common goals for your children. It will decrease the stress child rearing brings to a relationship, increase your effectiveness with your children, and allow you to enjoy your family.

Child-Rearing Questions

Put up your parenting goals where you can see them every day:

- What are the areas of child rearing where you and your partner agree?
- What are the areas of child rearing where you and your partner disagree?
- How is your relationship with each of your children?
- Do your children talk with you about important matters?
- Are you good at catching your children being good?
- Do you only notice them when they are out of line?
- Do you parent in ways similar or dissimilar to your own parents?

PROBLEM SOLVING

Too often poor problem-solving skills cause serious difficulties in relationships. When problems arise many people get caught up in their anger toward one another rather than taking a problem-solving approach to their disagreements.

No one teaches us how to solve relationship problems, so we are often left with ineffective or inappropriate ways of solving our disagreements with those we love. Without proper forethought, we often solve problems in relationships the same way our parents did. In a sense, they programmed our brains to respond automatically to specific situations. For example, a man whose father responded to arguments by walking away from them is likely to do the same thing. A woman whose mother responded to a disagreement by withholding affection is likely to pick that option when disagreements come up.

To avoid these unconscious (and mostly unhelpful) ways of problem solving, here is a simple formula that many of my patients have found helpful in resolving relational difficulties. It has been used between marital couples, between parents and children, and in relationships at work.

Basic Attitude

First, it is critical to have a baseline attitude of care and respect, and then to filter information about the other person through that attitude—having positive basic assumptions toward the other person. Simply believing that they care about you cuts down on the number of problems in relationships. When we get caught expecting the worst from another person, we often unconsciously set it up to get just what we expect. Expect the best.

Problem Definition

Second, when you encounter a problem with another person and begin feeling angry or upset, tell yourself to take a few deep breaths and monitor your thoughts for a moment. Next, ask yourself what the real issues are in the situation. What is the problem? Try to be as specific as possible.

Clarify Your Position and the Other Person's Position

Third, clarify your position to yourself about the issue with which you are dealing. If necessary, write it down. Fourth, ask the other person to clarify his or her position, and really try to understand things from their point of view.

Options, Decision and Monitoring

Fifth, together list the options available to help you resolve the situation. List as many options as you can think of, even if they sound ludicrous or silly. Sixth, together choose an option and then monitor how it turns out. If one fails, return to your list and choose another option.

Some of my patients post this problem-solving scheme where they can see it easily. Then, when a problem arises, they can go through the steps systematically to solve the immediate situation.

Here are two examples of how this problem-solving approach can be used:

A single father and his sixteen-year-old son often argued over the son's weekend curfew. Prior to discovering the problem-solving steps, they would yell at each other, and the father often grounded the son for the weekend. Both father and son felt terrible. When they tried this method, however, they were able to solve the problem.

It was easy to get them to agree that they cared about each other and wanted a close relationship; they wanted to have a positive attitude toward each other. They were able to be clear on what the problem was— how late the son stayed out on weekend nights. The son's position was that he should be able to stay out until midnight without calling home. The father, who remembered the things he did as a teenager when he was out late, wanted him home at ten o'clock. They had many options for solving this problem: they could both disagree and continue to be unhappy; they could compromise on a time in between 10 p.m. and midnight; the son could call and check in more frequently; or the father could accompany his son with his friends on the weekends (neither liked that option). They chose the option of an 11 p.m. curfew with the son calling home at least once by 10 p.m. Both parties made some concessions, and the father still felt he could supervise his son. They were to continue to monitor this agreement over two months' time to see if it worked satisfactorily.

While I was writing this book, my wife and I disagreed over our new Chevrolet Suburban. We had arranged to meet my brother and his family in the mountains around Lake Tahoe for a weekend of snow sledding and skiing. I wanted to take our new four-wheel drive vehicle to the mountains, feeling that safety was exactly the reason we bought this $30,000 vehicle. My wife, on the other hand, wanted to take our older mini-van to the snow, feeling she didn't want to slush up our new Suburban. I hate new vehicles. I stress over them until they have at least three scratches on them. We were both determined to have our way until we sat down and "problem-solved" the situation. We had no question that we care about each other, but it is always a good idea to check our attitudes. The problem was that we disagreed on the best vehicle to take to the snow. My position was that we bought the Suburban for safety and fun. The four-wheel drive and the vehicle's large size filled both requirements. In addition, I loved the Suburban's heater. My wife's position was that the vehicle was brand new (less than a month old); it would get dirty in the snow; accidents are more frequent in slippery conditions; and that our children and their cousins would get their dirty boots all over the new carpets and seats (some fortune-telling on her part). She just wanted to keep it looking new for several months. After all, we had saved a long time for it. We listed the potential options: take the Suburban, don't take the Suburban, take the Suburban and put plastic bags over the carpets and seats, rent another vehicle to take to the snow, make an agreement to have the carpet and seats of the new Suburban steam-cleaned if any harm came to them, stay home. We chose the option of taking the Suburban and agreeing to have it professionally cleaned if any harm came to it. None did.

Whenever you take a problem-solving approach you make important relationships stronger, because both people feel that they have had a chance to express their opinions and contribute to the solution.

RELATIONAL FOCUS STATEMENT:

Attitude and Assumptions: I make positive basic assumptions about my partner in an encouraging, supportive, and positive atmosphere.

Time: We spend daily special time together; some of the best time of our week is spent together; we compromise and alternate choosing how we spend our time together.

Communication: We have two-way communication that is active, persistent, clear, and positive.

Child Rearing: As parents we are involved, open, firm, together, kind, and fun; for our children we act in a way to help them be relational, responsible, independent, self-confident, self-accepting, adaptable, emotionally free, and fun.

Problem Solving: We are able to solve problems in an attitude of care and respect by taking time to define the problem, clearly state our differing positions, understand the issues from the other person's point of view, list our options, make a decision, and then monitor the outcome.

Chapter 9
Shared Bonding, Affection, and Physical Love Focus:
Bonding, emotional bridges, and sexual and nonsexual touching

Physical connection is a critical element of the parent-infant bonding process. With caressing, kissing, sweet words, and loving eye contact from the mother or father, the baby becomes able to feel pleasure, love, trust, and security. The baby begins to sense a bond or connectedness to the parents. Without touching, kissing, affectionate words, or loving looks from parents, the baby never learns trust, begins to feel lonely and insecure, and becomes irritable and unresponsive.

The reaction of the baby to the parent is almost equally important in this parent-infant bonding equation. When parents give affection to their infant, but the infant does not respond or becomes irritable with the attempt to show love, parents may unconsciously begin to lessen the amount of love they give to the infant. Bonding is a two-way street. The parents, misreading the situation, often feel hurt and rejected, as if something were wrong with them as parents. Psychiatrists used to label mothers of autistic children cold because they were less responsive than other mothers. Numerous research studies have shown, however, that the mothers became more reserved because they were getting no reciprocation or positive feedback from the children. Reciprocal love and affection is critical to making the parent-infant bond work.

Adult love is similar. For proper bonding to occur, intimate couples need holding, kissing, sweet words, and affectionate eye contact. Without physical love, an intimate relationship often sours, and one or both partners withdraw, become irritable, or begin to look elsewhere for love. Physical manifestations of love need to be reciprocated or the other partner feels hurt or rejected, causing the bond to erode.

In this chapter, you will ask yourself and your partner what you want from your physical love together. I will ask you to examine: your bond with each other, your preconceived notions and programming about touching and physical love, your automatic thoughts about sex, your desires, and the desires of your partner. In addition, I will teach you how to provide the best bonding environment and opportunities for loving each other.

LIMBIC BONDING

What is the condition of the physical bond with your partner right now? Are you in tune with each other? Do you feel solidly connected? Or do you feel out of sync? Is tension pulling you apart? Do you feel alone when you are together? Is your bond increasing in strength the longer you are together? Or is it weakening from a lack of attention? As I mentioned, reciprocal physical bonding is critical to a relationship.

The limbic system of your brain is involved with bonding. The limbic system is located at the center of the brain (in the primitive part of the brain), and it is about the size of a walnut. Scientists have observed that when an animal's limbic system is abnormal, the maternal-infant bonding process is impaired.

Besides bonding, the limbic system regulates your mood, stores highly charged emotional memories, modulates libido or sexual energy, and directly processes your sense of smell. In fact, your sense of smell is the only one of the five senses that is processed directly into the limbic system, which is why smells and scents evoke such powerful emotional responses. The multibillion-dollar perfume and deodorant industries are built on this principle. Beautiful smells evoke wonderful emotions, offensive smells cause people to feel negative and to withdraw.

A friend of mine told me that English Leather Cologne always does the trick with his wife. Even when she is mad at him, the smell of English Leather relaxes and excites her; she is more likely to forget her anger and become more affectionate (an important observation for him to make). Look for ways to increase your bond with your partner on a daily basis by creating the best fragrances in the environment.

List the smells you like most about your partner (share them).

As the limbic system stores highly charged emotional memories, the couple's history together is also intimately connected to the bonding process. The more positive experiences you have shared, the closer the bond. The more hard times you have experienced as a couple the weaker the bond. It depends on how you weathered the hard times as a couple. Strong bonds grow through adversity, weak bonds are often shattered by trouble.

Ariel and Phillip had been married for fourteen years when their pastor sent them to see me. They were on the verge of splitting up. Phillip had been caught having an affair with Ariel's best friend, Jackie, who was going through a divorce. Ariel was angry, hurt, and afraid. She had had so many good times with Phillip that she couldn't believe he would jeopardize their marriage. Through counseling they were able to understand the reasons for the affair, which included Ariel's frequent business trips that left Phillip feeling isolated and left behind, Phillip turning forty and wondering if he was still attractive, and Jackie's seductiveness due to her need for an emotional connection during a painful divorce. Despite Ariel's hurt feelings, she was able to forgive Phillip and work through her pain. She said, "We've had such great times. He deserves another chance."

Renee and Steve were a different story. They had only been married for two years when their relationship fell apart. It had been a stormy relationship almost since it began. Renee was pregnant when they got married and the relationship was always under some sort of pressure, including family pressure, financial pressure, and pressure from having a child before they had time to bond as a couple. So when Steve caught Renee having an affair, he packed his bags, left, and filed for divorce within the month.

Bonding in relationships is enhanced by a history of happy times together and great fragrances. Bonding is also enhanced by passion. Since the limbic system is also involved with modulating libido, sexuality is important in the adult bonding process. Passionate love and ecstasy often provide the glue for an intimate relationship. The acts of caressing, kissing, touching, fondling, squeezing, and loving record powerful chemical memory traces in your brain that connect you to the other person. As our brain works through association, pleasurable memory traces associated to the person you love enhance the bonding process. It is such a warm feeling to think about the wonderful love you and your partner shared the night before.

Positive memory traces encourage you to think about your partner, call him or her, and do other things to connect with him or her during the day. The strength of these memory tracings is proportional to the intensity of passion. The better the experience, the more powerful the memories. This is one of the reasons it is so important to have a healthy, passionate, fun, sexual relationship. The bond that keeps you together during difficult times in part depends on the passionate memory tracings you carry around in your head as you go through your day.

Negative memory traces erode the bond. Be careful how you treat your partner, because the brain's memory system stores most interactions. If you spend a lot of time rejecting the advances of your partner, the memory traces will be of rejection. If you hurry lovemaking, the memory traces will be that you did not have enough time for intimacy. If you belittle or ridicule your partner during lovemaking, he or she will have painful memory traces and will avoid you.

What memory traces are being laid down in your limbic system with regards to your sexual relationship? What memory traces are you encouraging to be laid down in the limbic system of your partner?

Your sexual relationship matters in many ways. I often ask couples to develop a library of passionate memories. I have them write out the ten best passionate times they had with each other. Visiting this library (dwelling on the best times) can really help the relationship when times are hard.

On a separate piece of paper, list the ten best passionate times you have had with your partner. Share them with your partner, and look for opportunities to add great, new times to your list.

This limbic bonding process is the reason that casual or friendly sex doesn't work. Sex enhances emotional bonding, and when two people have sex just for the fun of it, one person will form an attachment and end up getting hurt. Anne was feeling sexually ignored at home. She felt that she was a woman with a high sexual drive, but her husband was either working or too tired to make love with her as often as she liked. Many guys flirted with her, but she had always been faithful. Out of frustration she began having an affair with a co-worker with whom she had been friends for several years. It was just going to be friendly sex, they agreed, just for fun and pleasure. It worked that way for two months. But, then Anne began to get more and more attached to her lover. The more attached she became, the more he pulled away. Anne ended up feeling used. Respect the concept of limbic bonding, and use it to draw closer to your mate.

PRECONCEIVED NOTIONS ABOUT SEX

What were your preconceived notions about sex?

What were the messages about sex you received as a child? Who was the first person to tell you about the "birds and the bees?" What was/is your mother's attitude toward sex? What was/is your father's attitude toward sex? Was nudity something to be ashamed of in your house, or were you taught that your body was special? As a teenager, what was your opinion about your body? What is your opinion now about your body? How would your partner answer these questions? Share this information together in an environment of empathy and active listening.

Preconceived ideas from the past affect every aspect of life, especially sex. The messages you received from parents, brothers, sisters, and friends play a role in your day-to-day sex life as an adult. If sex was thought of as something dirty, you will have trouble discarding the feeling that you are doing something bad, though your rational mind believes otherwise. If sex was forbidden, you will have trouble saying yes, even when you feel desire. If sex was something to hide and lie about, you will have trouble making love in the light of day. If sex was used as a way of showing and giving love to your mate, you will feel good about using it to show love and affection.

Here is a list of some of the harmful and helpful preconceived messages about sexuality.

Harmful Messages About Sex:
- sex is dirty
- sex is forbidden
- sex is only for procreation
- sex should always be performed the same way
- a woman should never be the aggressor
- there is something wrong with a naked body
- nakedness is associated with the feeling of shame
- sex is for the pleasure of a man
- a woman who enjoys sex is a slut
- you are a man when you score with a woman
- a real man has had lots of sex partners
- if you love me you will do what I want you to do

Helpful Messages About Sex:

- in the right context, sex is wonderful
- sex is for pleasure, bonding, and procreation
- sex enhances the bond between committed partners
- there are many ways to express sexuality
- sex is important to an intimate relationship
- men and women need to ask for what they want
- nakedness is beautiful if you are comfortable with it
- your masculinity (or femininity) is defined not by the number of your sexual partners, but by your ability to care for yourself and others
- if you love me you will listen to my needs and work it out with me

How people think about sexuality in America has shifted radically over the past five decades. Sexuality has gone from the marital bedroom in the fifties, to the stage and movie screen in the early sixties, to the grass at Woodstock where people "loved the one they were with" in the late sixties, to "whomever you happen to be living with" in the seventies and early eighties, back to the confines of a monogamous relationship with the onset of AIDS in the middle eighties and nineties. Parents are more confused now than ever on the best ways to educate their children about sexuality. Most parents avoid equating sex outside of marriage with the fires of hell, but they are teaching their teenagers about the dangers of AIDS and the need for thoughtfulness about sex.

Explore your own preconceived notions about sex, then get rid of the notion that wonderful sex is somehow outside the bounds of biblical teaching. In the context of marriage, sexuality is a gift of pleasure and bonding. Here are several verses from the Song of Solomon (found in the Old Testament between the books of Ecclesiastes and Isaiah) to illustrate this point.

- "Let him kiss me with the kisses of his mouth— for his love is more delightful than wine."
- "Pleasing is the fragrance of your perfumes; your

name is like perfume poured out." (Solomon knew the principle of smells and the limbic system.)

- "Your stature is like that of the palm, and your breasts like clusters of fruit."
- "I said I will climb the palm tree; I will take hold of its fruit."
- "May your breasts be like the clusters of the vine, the fragrance of your breath like apples."
- "My love burns like a blazing fire, like a mighty flame."
- "I am a wall, and my breasts are like towers. Thus I have become in his eyes, like one bringing contentment."

Biblically speaking, sex is intended for pleasure, bonding, and procreation.

PROGRAMMING, EMOTIONAL BRIDGES, AND SEX

Understand and redirect programming from the past. Over the years I have treated many men for premature ejaculation. Frequently, men with premature ejaculation have a past incident or series of incidents relating to failure. For example, I treated a man named Joe who was having problems with premature ejaculation. Joe had tried the standard remedies without success, and he was considering a penile implant to help him maintain an erection. Joe's wife was against the surgery, but she was also frustrated by the lack of satisfying sex in their life.

In taking his history, I asked Joe about the first time he had sex. He told me that it was when he was seventeen years old. Joe had wanted to take out this girl for several months and he was excited when she agreed. After several dates, they became sexually active and found themselves starting intercourse. It was over in a matter of seconds. Joe was so humiliated that he never asked this girl out again, though she seemed to understand and didn't embarrass him.

During their twenty-two-year marriage, almost every time Joe and his wife tried to have intercourse, it ended quickly. He wept with frustration during my first interview with him. He felt he had failed with his wife, and he was afraid of losing her love and approval. Under hypnosis I asked him to explain the feelings and thoughts he had during intercourse. He said, "I almost always predict failure. I'm so worried it won't work that it usually doesn't. I feel like a failure, that it will never be right."

While he was still in the hypnotic trance, I asked him to go back to the first time he had ever had feelings and thoughts of failure (making an emotional bridge with the emotion at the time of the premature ejaculation—failure). He then retold me about what happened to him when he was seventeen years old. Suspecting more, I asked him to go back even further in his life, maybe to a time when he was a young child. He started to cry (much like during our initial interview). He told me of an encounter with his father when he was five years old. "I was having real trouble learning how to read. Later on I was diagnosed with dyslexia, a reading/learning disability. My father was so frustrated with me that he called me a failure and he said I'd never be able to succeed. I think he told me that a lot until the doctor told him I had a problem. I was devastated. I knew I'd never be like the rest of the kids."

Joe told me he hadn't thought about the interactions with his father in many years, but his father's message still rang clear in his head. "You're a failure. You'll never be able to succeed." And even though he succeeded in his career, sexually he had always had problems. Under hypnosis I had him correct the negative programming, told him he was a success no matter what happened sexually, and suggested that he predict wonderful sex with his wife. In the span of two months, the premature ejaculation was gone. He didn't need surgery. He needed to correct erroneous messages from his past, and he needed to believe he was going to be successful.

What are your emotional bridges to the past regarding sex. What feelings and thoughts from the past are triggered by current events. Your past, unless you seek to understand it, often controls your sexual behavior. Here is another example. Karen, age thirty-six, was well until about a year before she saw me. All of a sudden she stopped making love with her husband. She began to feel depressed and anxious. She started avoiding friends and going out by herself. Her husband called her a neat freak, because she spent inordinate amounts of time cleaning, which was a change for her over the past year. She became especially anxious when she would see a bug or feel something sticky on a counter or table. She went from doctor to doctor trying to figure out the problem.

In taking a history, I asked her what she felt inside whenever she felt something sticky. She said it made her feel dirty and creepy, which is why she stopped having intercourse with her husband. I then asked her if there was an event that made her feel that way the year before when she first started to avoid sex. She suddenly remembered that her house became infested with small black bugs, and it was weeks before she and her husband were free of them. This was an important connection. I then asked her to go back to the first time she had felt dirty and creepy. She then tearfully told me of her poor childhood when her family lived in rundown apartments that were often infested with bugs. She remembered one occasion when she woke up to find hundreds of crickets crawling on her head. Initially, in the office she became more anxious. But as she told me her childhood horror stories, she began to relax. She was beginning to connect her present fear of bugs and stickiness with events from her childhood. Through this connection she was able to get them out of the realm of her unconscious and into the present where she could face her fears from an adult perspective. Therapeutically, she could begin to soothe the little girl inside her and reassure her that things were different now. She then was able to make love with her husband without feeling dirty or creepy.

Building emotional bridges to past feelings is often essential in understanding current sexual behavior. We do not generally travel on these bridges to the past by choice. Rather, our passage on them is triggered by something in the present that reminds us of events or people in the past. For example, when a wife perceives a look from her husband as critical, she may flash back to a time when her father disapproved of her. Thus, the wife might spend the rest of the day feeling sad because she returned to a time when she felt bad.

Travel on these emotional bridges occurs at the speed of light. A person might be having a great day, and then something small occurs that turns the rest of the day into a disaster. People who have been raped or abused often travel on these bridges back to the abuse without being aware of it. Anything in the present that vaguely reminds them of the abuse can trigger a panic attack or an incredible sense of dread.

Only by recognizing our bridges to the past can we gain some control over them. What bridges do you travel on? Are they helpful for you? An important technique that I used with Karen in the example above, was for her to ask herself when she first remembered having the feeling that was bothering her. When you do this and you understand that incident, ask yourself to go back further into your childhood to see if those feelings existed then. Childhood is often the emotional source for negative or difficult feelings. But once they are recognized, people can begin to work with the feelings or events from a more adult or rational perspective, thus taking away their power.

Some sexual emotional bridges to the past need to be blown up; they are not helpful. These involve those bridges that make us feel guilt, shame, sadness, and anger. These emotions have no useful purpose. Some sexual bridges need to be widened and enhanced; they help give us life and hope. It is important to remember positive, happy times from the past. They bring smiles to our faces and lightness to our hearts. Spend some time each day traveling on a bridge to a wonderful, sexual memory. Also, spend time each day building new uplifting sexual memories that you will be able to travel back to in the future.

GETTING RID OF THE A.N.T.s IN YOUR BED

Along with bonding and programming from the past, moment-by-moment thoughts play a critical role in affection and sexuality. As discussed in the chapter on automatic negative thoughts, thoughts instantaneously affect every part of your body. Whenever you have a positive thought, your brain releases chemicals that make your whole body feel good; whenever you have a disappointed, angry, or depressing thought, your brain releases chemicals that make your body feel tense. Because of their high concentration of nerve fibers, your sexual organs are sensitive to the quality of your thoughts. Wonderful thoughts stimulate physical excitement, negative thoughts can turn you off in an instant.

If your goal is to have a healthy, pleasurable, and stimulating sex life as a couple, you must monitor your thinking patterns. Clearly, some thoughts help your sex life, and some thoughts ruin it. Eradicating the a.n.t.s in your sexual life will enhance its quality immediately.

A.n.t.s can invade your mind and bed at any time. To rid yourself of these pests, you must notice when they occur, identify them as false, and immediately talk back to them. Here are examples of a.n.t.s that infest sexuality.

1. *"Always" thinking:* thinking in words such as "always," "all," "never," "no one," "everyone," "every time," "everything."

- "You always turn me down."
- "Every time we make love, it is on your timing."
- "All you want is one thing."
- "You never touch me the way I want to be touched."

- "I am always approaching you; you never approach me."
- "You never listen to my needs."

2. *Focusing on the negative:* only seeing the bad in a situation.
- "It was great, but it won't last."
- "Even though we had a great evening, you ignored me when we came home. You just went to sleep after we had such an intimate time together."
- "You've never had multiple orgasms."

3. *Fortune-telling:* predicting the worst possible outcome to a situation.
- "I know you won't be interested in me."
- "I won't last long."
- "You won't do what I like."
- "You'll be too tired."
- "You won't be satisfied."

4. *Mind-reading:* believing that you know what another person is thinking even though they haven't told you.
- "You really aren't interested."
- "You're not turned on by me."
- "You don't care about my feelings."
- "You must want someone else."
- "You don't like how I look."

5. *Thinking with your feelings:* believing the thoughts behind negative feelings are the truth without ever questioning them. Feelings are based on complex programming and bridges from the past and may have little to do with what is actually true. Recognize your negative feelings and the associated negative thoughts.
- "I feel anxious when you look at my body, because I'm afraid I don't turn you on."
- "I feel like I want to hide because I know you think I'm fat, ugly, and unattractive."
- "Every time we make love and you then fall

asleep, I feel abandoned and used."
- "I feel you don't want me."
- "I feel sad in bed with you; that must mean you don't care about me."

6. *Guilt beatings:* thinking in words such as "should," "must," "ought to," or "have to."
- "You ought to make love to me."
- "I have to fake an orgasm so he'll be satisfied."
- "I shouldn't be playful during lovemaking."
- "I must not enjoy sex."
- "She should have an orgasm if she loves me."

7. *Labeling:* attaching a negative label to yourself or to someone else.
- "You're cold."
- "You're a sex maniac."
- "You're pushy."
- "You're fat."
- "You're a prude."

8. *Personalization:* Innocuous events are taken to have personal meaning.
- "You didn't touch me today; you must be mad at me."
- "You don't seem interested, it must be me."
- "You finished too quickly, I must have done something wrong."
- "Your headache must be my fault."

9. *Blame:* blaming someone else for the problems you have.
- "If you weren't so insistent, then we wouldn't have problems."
- "It's your fault we're having problems."
- "If you'd pay attention to me at other times, our sex life would be better."
- "You don't think about my needs."
- "If you'd do something differently, we wouldn't have problems."

These a.n.t.s erode sexuality and interfere with closeness between a couple. Be on guard for negative thoughts and eradicate them whenever you can. The best way I have found to get rid of these thoughts is to write them down, identify them as erroneous, and talk back to them. You don't have to believe every thought that goes through your head. If you don't recognize and eradicate these thoughts, however, they will control you completely. For example, when you think, "He won't be interested in me," you believe it, become irritated by the thought, and then act as if it were true. Your negative behavior then causes him not to be interested in you. If, on the other hand, you think he might be interested in you, you will act in a much more positive way and enhance your chances of gaining his interest.

Recognizing and responding back to negative thoughts is only part of the strategy for establishing the best thoughts on love. A more powerful strategy to enhance your sexuality as a couple is to develop and infuse stimulating thoughts about the relationship. Exciting thoughts are stimulated by wonderful smells, exciting sights, loving sounds, erotic tastes, and involve wonderful memories. Use your five senses to develop a series of images that turn you on. As you go through your day, think about the closest times you have shared together. Write them down. Have a special night every month where you just talk about your wonderful sexual times together. In large part, you are what you think; direct your sexual thoughts in ways that enhance closeness and togetherness in the relationship.

THERE ARE WAYS TO SAY THINGS AND THERE ARE WAYS TO SAY THINGS

How you express your thoughts is just as important as the thoughts themselves. Expression and communication can be clear and positive, or they can be infected with accusations and blame. For example, when you feel your partner is ignoring you sexually, you can choose how you tell them that. You can say,

"You don't care about me! You always ignore me. You're not interested in me. I'm so angry at you I wouldn't make love with you even if you approached me right now." Or you could say something like, "You're very special to me. I miss holding you. I need to touch you." Notice these markedly different ways of dealing with the same situation. Which way do you think is likely to be effective in obtaining love? Watch how you express your thoughts and desires. Be effective by playing the scene out in your head and evaluating how your partner is likely to respond before you open your mouth. Focus on the goal of your words.

YOUR DESIRES

What do you want from your sexuality? What are your needs, desires, and fantasies? If you could have everything you wanted, what would that be? How have your needs changed over the years? Are you able to communicate your desires clearly or do you expect that your partner should know what you want? Are you too inhibited to ask for what you want?

To understand your own needs better, it is often helpful to craft your desires among your five senses:

- What are your visual desires? What sights turn you on?
- What do you love hearing? What sounds excite you?
- What tastes linger in your mind? What tastes make your heart pound?
- How do you want to be touched? What feelings turn you on?
- What scents please you? What smells drive you wild?

Thinking about what turns you on gives you the opportunity to shape your desires into reality.

YOUR PARTNER'S DESIRES

Do you know what your partner wants from his or

her sexuality? Do you talk about her needs, desires, and fantasies? Are you tuned in to his interests? Do you know her body rhythms and cycles? Are you able to get outside of yourself to see his needs? How have her needs changed over the years? Is your partner able to clearly communicate his or her desires, or does he or she expect that you should know these wants? Is he or she too inhibited to ask you to fulfill those desires?

What is important for your sexual lives together? How do you want to be held, kissed, talked to, and looked at? How do you want to be made love to? How do you want to give love? It is important to discuss these issues.

Ask your partner about their wants and desires. Ask them how they would craft their desires with the five senses. Information and knowledge are power. Knowing yourself and your lover will strengthen your sexual relationship so that it will bring strength, joy, and pleasure to your entire relationship.

THE BEST ENVIRONMENT FOR PHYSICAL LOVE

On too many occasions, couples are derailed from passion by an environment that is hostile to love. Many couples have told me that just as they were warming up to each other, the circumstances in their household threw ice on them. For example, right before bed, the mom might get into a fight with one of the teenagers (this is a death blow to passion, at least passionate love). Dogs barking, phones ringing, and beepers going off are other examples of environmental hazards that need to be cleaned up to create an atmosphere conducive to love. The following is a list of turn-offs that impair physical bonding in a relationship. It is followed by a list of turn-ons that promote physical love and togetherness. I compiled these lists from friends, colleagues, patients, and personal experience.

"TURN-OFFS"

- hearing the children fighting in the next room

- receiving no attention from your mate until you both hop in the sack
- crude noises or gestures
- an automatic "this won't go any further" at the start of foreplay
- unclean or unshaven
- scratchy face or legs
- body odor
- bad breath
- deodorant powder you can taste
- the smell of mentholated rub on a chest
- a lack of playfulness, too serious
- criticism
- predicting failure
- making a partner feel guilty for not making love
- whining or being "too" pushy
- too much or distracting light
- witnessing your partner being cruel or hostile to others
- poor parenting skills
- showing incompetence at the job or at managing money
- insecurity
- anger (except for a few)
- a bad mood, irritability
- pain, headaches
- a negative attitude
- demanding sex (again, except for a few)
- commenting on or looking at the positive aspects of others
- intoxication
- a gunny sack for pajamas
- complaining
- lack of focus, distractions
- certain types of clothes (i.e., old sweat suits)
- cockiness, phoniness, flaunting behavior
- someone who blames others for the problems at hand
- a partner who has a cold or who is tired
- dogs barking or scratching to get in your room

- children at the door wanting to know why they can't come in
- routine
- sexual contact without any nonsexual contact
- a lack of foreplay or time loving
- no afterthoughts or afterglow (rolling over and falling asleep leaves a memory that says the moment was for sex only, not for love)

List your own turn-offs, and ask your partner to list their turn-offs.

TURN-OFFS

1. _____
   _____
2. _____
   _____
3. _____
   _____
4. _____
   _____
5. _____
   _____

TURN-ONS

- privacy
- quiet
- no noise from the kids
- talking, loving looks, and touching long before overt sexual contact
- romantic music
- gentle singing
- special touch
- romantic movies
- positive time together
- beautiful scents
- clean-shaven
- fresh breath
- playful attitude

- true listening
- talking about wonderful past experiences— mutual anticipation
- sexy clothes—special perfume or cologne
- favorite meal or dessert together
- sitting or lying in front of a fire
- a soothing drink—a clear focus on pleasure
- a soothing neck, back, or foot massage— opportunity to shower or bathe together
- multiple sensual excitements
- lengthy foreplay and unhurried love
- a lingering enjoyment of the moment after love (rolling over and falling asleep leaves a memory that says the moment was for sex alone, not for love)
- seeing your partner be competent at work
- self-confidence without cockiness
- certain looks that say, "I like what I see"
- watching your partner be helpful and thoughtful to others
- seeing your partner be a wonderful mom or dad with the children
- acts of kindness and thoughtfulness
- keeping in touch during the day through phone calls and notes
- a beautiful room
- the way your partner dresses (or undresses)
- the way clothes fit
- certain types of clothes (white shirts and ties, fancy shoes, tight sweaters, nylons, etc.)
- an openness to experimentation without preconceived judgments

List your own turn-ons, and ask your partner to list his or her turn-ons.

1. _____
   _____
2. _____
   _____

3. _____
   _____

4. _____
   _____

5. _____
   _____

Design the best environment for physical love, incorporating each of your five senses. Be aware of and discuss your turn-offs and turn-ons and your partner's. Always try to focus on the positive. Look for ways to incorporate the turn-ons into your sexual relationship and eliminate the turn-offs.

Another important aspect in the environment of love is time, actual physical time together. I have known many couples who truly love each other's company. But the pace of their lives prevents them from connecting. One couple told me they were just too busy to make love. They said when they made love it was wonderful and they asked themselves why they didn't connect more often. Physical love needs to be made a priority. It often reflects the quality of the relationship. To that end, I ask my patients who are managers or computer buffs to obtain project management software and to consider their love lives as separate projects that require investments of time and skill.

Watch for sexual cycles in a relationship. Many couples tell me that their relationship goes through many different cycles. When one person is feeling amorous, the other one may be tired or drained. Tammy was feeling this way. When she first came to see me she complained that her husband didn't pay enough attention to her. She wanted more sex and more touching. When I taught her to ask for what she wanted, her husband was responsive. In fact, he was so interested in Tammy that she began to lose interest. Six months later Tammy found the situation had reversed. Her husband wanted her all the time and she felt suffocated. When you suspect that your partner is feeling crowded by your advances, back off slightly to give them some breathing room. That may actually help to bring them back.

PHYSICAL LOVE FOCUS STATEMENT

Here is an example of a clear goal statement for this area of your relationship. Make your own to fit the needs of your relationship.

We seek excitement, passion, and sensuality in an atmosphere of fun and mutual giving. We will include lots of nonsexual and sexual touching to promote connectedness and bonding.

Chapter 10
Shared Fun Focus:
Fun and Laughter

When was the last time you and your partner laughed together?

When was the last time you found your partner interesting, exciting, or playful?

When was the last time he or she found you interesting, exciting, or playful?

How long has it been since you and your partner got away together just to enjoy each other's company?

If you are too busy to have fun together, then you are too busy.

Many people are so busy making money or focusing on their careers that they lose perspective on what is important. Including fun as part of the culture in a relationship will help keep it healthy and strong. Too many couples are trapped by the day-to-day drudgery that dominates their lives. Laundry, cooking, cleaning, homework, transporting children, cleaning up after pets, yard work, keeping the cars running, and paying bills are just a few of the repetitive chores that drain energy, fun, and freshness for couples. Ruts often ruin relationships by causing boredom and staleness, which places the relationship at risk for infidelities.

Jo Ellen and Bill were on the verge of separating when they first came to see me. They had been angry at each other for six years, ever since the birth of their first child. Before that they were madly in love during a four-year courtship and the first four years of their marriage. They spent many weekends skiing, hiking, camping, and going to concerts and plays. They had loved reading to each other, playing board games together, and giving each other back rubs and massages. This changed when Jo Ellen became pregnant with their first child. She had morning sickness for the first four months of the pregnancy and never felt well throughout. After the baby was born, she had post-partum depression, or baby blues, for three months and continually pushed aside all of Bill's efforts to have fun with her. Since the baby was their first, Jo Ellen worried about all the problems new moms worry about. She was up nearly every night for several hours in the middle of the night and she felt "tired all the time." Six months later, Jo Ellen was pregnant again.

Both Jo Ellen and Bill began to resign themselves to a different lifestyle, and they never went out alone together. Bill had given up trying to woo Jo Ellen and he found more pleasure in playing tennis and drinking beer with his friends after work. Bill began looking at other women, and he longed for some affection and attention. One day they had a terrible fight as Bill was getting ready to leave to go to the tennis club. Bill said he was so unhappy that he wasn't going to come home. Jo Ellen told him to stay away because there hadn't been any happiness in their home for years. That night after his tennis match, Bill found himself asking an attractive woman at the club out for a drink. She agreed. The whole time they were together, Bill felt guilty and alone and he missed Jo Ellen. What had happened to their relationship, he wondered? They had been so good together, now they were almost history. He politely told this woman that he couldn't stay and went to his office. He called my office asking for help.

As he related their story, it became clear that this couple had lost themselves in their busy lives. The children had disturbed their equilibrium, and they had never recovered their sense of themselves as a couple, separate from the children. They had become oblivious to the idea of fun and excitement and were trapped in the drudgery of everyday living. I encouraged Bill to bring in Jo Ellen to work on their marriage. The guilt he felt when he was with this other woman was important. It indicated to him that he needed to seek help rather than damage the relationship.

I often start therapy with couples by asking them how they met and what attracted them to each other. Both Jo Ellen and Bill talked about how much fun they had during their courtship and the first four years of their marriage. They both missed it dearly but didn't know how to get the fun back. I told them to start with thirty minutes a day of mandatory adult fun time, playing a game, giving a back rub, reading to each other, doing a puzzle together. I made it clear that I meant the time was *mandatory*. Without a good relationship between them, there would be no family. Nothing was more important than their relationship. I also told them that they needed to have at least one date a week without the children, doing something fun, such as attending a concert, going to a movie, going hiking, going to a special restaurant, or taking a long drive.

At first they both said that they couldn't find the time or the babysitters to do this every week. I asked them what was really important in their lives. Was their marriage a priority or was it relegated to the end of their line of energy? They got the message. After two weeks they made their daily mandatory adult fun time and weekly date a priority. "It made all the difference," Bill told me. "We always really liked each other's company; we just had to spend a little unpressured time together to remember how much we missed each other." Jo Ellen continued, "Even though we love our children dearly, we needed some adult time away from them. Before we started therapy, I felt as if I should be with them all the time and felt guilty about doing adult things. I can see now how burned out I was getting."

An essential part of having fun as a couple is being able to laugh together. Laughter is healing, for individuals and couples. Norman Cousins, in his best-selling book, *The Anatomy of an Illness,* relayed the story of how he cured his own incurable illness, ankylosing spondylitis (where the cells in your own body attack your joints), with laughter. Doctors gave him little hope for a cure using conventional treatments. Cousins decided not to leave the fate of his health in a medical system that offered little hope, and he searched for answers. His answer was locking himself in a hotel room and watching hundreds of hours of comedies. He laughed until he healed. Weeks later his illness improved; months later it was gone.

Laughter also heals relationships. I treated a couple engaged in a power struggle. Each of them had to be right, no matter what the situation. They were irritable with each other and had little fun together. During one of our sessions, they told me about the impact a funny movie had on their relationship. *Grumpy Old Men* with Walter Mathau and Jack Lemmon was the comedy. After the movie, they talked and laughed about it for hours. They enjoyed the humor and felt close sharing the one-liners. They shared wonderful sex that night. They had such fun that they went back to see the movie the next night and the next, and they made love each night. I gave them the homework of seeing a comedy a week. It worked for them. They had something fun to share and felt close when they laughed together. Laughter was healing. In my house, we have a large collection of "Mash" television shows. Whenever things get tense, watching an old episode of "Mash" with Hawkeye, Trapper, B.J., Klinger, Hot Lips, or Frank (the lipless wonder) can make everyone feel good and relaxed enough to deal with the tension in a more constructive fashion.

Fun, freshness, and laughter are essential for a healthy relationship. Do you spend fun time regularly with your partner? Make fun and laughter a priority in your relationship to keep it alive, healthy, and fresh.

WORKSHEET ON FUN

Having fun in a relationship is key to its survival. Fun and pleasure keep a relationship young and enhance a couple's ability to enjoy each other. Often, while couples are stuck in the day-to-day grind, they forget that one of the reasons they are working is so that they can take time to enjoy their lives together. Instructions: Answer the following questions in private. Then come together, share your answers, and listen to the other person before you respond to their answers. Take turns going first on each question.

1. Fun Activities. Rank the areas of fun you have in your life in the order of their importance to you (1 = most important, 17 = least important).

    ___ Individual (individual hobbies, crafts, reading, etc.)

    ___ Cultural (plays, operas, museums, music, etc.)

    ___ Movies

    ___ Shopping

    ___ Collecting (antiques, cars, stamps, etc.)

    ___ Athletics participation (golf, weightlifting, aerobics, etc.)

    ___ Thrill seeking (skydiving, kayaking, driving in New York, etc.)

    ___ Athletics spectator

    ___ Outdoor recreation (boating, hiking, beaches, etc.)

    ___ Games

    ___ Activities with children

    ___ Taking drives

    ___ Eating out

    ___ Community events (parades, celebrations, craft fairs, etc.)

    ___ Traveling (local)

    ___ Traveling (new places)

    ___ Traveling (old haunts)

2. How much fun are you currently having together?

3. What activities do you do where you have the most fun together?

4. What do you do for fun individually?

5. What do you do for fun with others outside this relationship?

6. List three people who you know that have the most fun in their lives? What are they doing that gives you this idea?

7. List the ten times in your life that you had the most fun?

8. What five fun things would you like to do that you have never done?

9. What are the areas of fun you have in common?

10. How much time do you want to devote to fun? (Don't shortchange your life. There is solid research that suggests that including a healthy portion of fun may actually prolong your life!)
- together:
- with others:
- individually:

11. Fun Goals (given the information above what would you like in each area listed below):
- together:
- with others:
- individually:

SHARED FUN FOCUS STATEMENT

Fun, freshness, and laughter are priorities in our relationship. We realize that these things are essential to health and make life's problems a lot easier to handle together. We actively look for ways to contribute lightheartedness and good fun to the relationship.

Chapter 11
Shared Work Focus:
Home, job/career

One of the keys to turmoil or happiness in a relationship is how the couple handles the day-to-day aspects of work. Work, both inside and outside the home, is a very emotional issue. It encompasses the concepts of fairness, sharing, self-worth, dignity, and meaning. Work either brings a couple closer or drives them further apart. There is no middle ground.

WORK CAN BRING A COUPLE TOGETHER

Work brings a couple closer together when it is shared, adds meaning to the lives of the couple, and helps make their lives together run more smoothly. Work can be a tremendously positive force in a relationship. Ned and Kelly understood the concept of work and used it to their advantage. Ned was a physician who had gone through three different office managers. The first one was scattered and disorganized; the second manager had trouble getting along with Ned's associate; and the third one stole from Ned. When Ned asked his wife Kelly if she would help out until he could find a replacement, she was hesitant. Their friends had counseled them against working together. "Working marriages don't work," they said. Ned and Kelly, however, had the same goals and respected each other's efforts. After she came on as Ned's temporary office manager, Kelly truly began to understand the pressure her husband was under in his medical practice. Ned increased the amount of work he did around the house and began to appreciate all that Kelly did to keep the household and the kids on track. They also saw a lot more of each other since they shared work and often ate lunches together. They became a team with the same goals. They felt the situation was working so well that they made it permanent. Ned never treated Kelly as an employee, but as a partner. Before they worked together, Kelly had felt somewhat inferior to Ned. He was a highly respected doctor in the community, and she "just took care of the home and kids." Working with Ned gave Kelly a sense of importance and togetherness. It made a big difference in their relationship.

WHAT EVER HAPPENED TO THE DONNA REED GENERATION?

Work also can be a tremendously negative force in a relationship. Differing purposes and miscommunication can cause turmoil that damages the relationship. Betty's job caused her to travel a great deal. She was gone for virtually two weeks out of every month. Initially, her husband, Frank, was pleased that Betty had landed a good job. He was willing to help, and he had ideas on how they could spend the extra money. But Frank had no idea how much work it took to care for two elementary school age children and a household. On weeks when Betty was away, he got up an hour earlier to get the children ready for school. Some mornings his youngest child dawdled, making them a couple minutes late. He then commuted forty minutes to work (in heavier traffic due to the later start). He frequently felt hurried at work, because he had to leave on time to get to the day-care center before they closed. Feeling tired after picking up the kids, he then had to fix dinner, help with homework, get the kids ready for bed, and clean up the house. By the time the children were asleep, he was too tired to read or to do anything he enjoyed except crawl into bed himself. After eight months of this pace, he didn't care about the extra money; he just wanted a prolonged rest.

Betty was smitten by the world of business. She was successful at her job and was being promoted within her company. After years of "just raising the children," she felt valued and important. Working boosted her self-esteem. When Frank started complaining about the work at home, Betty became defensive. She reminded him that he had promised to support her and that she had done all of those tasks at home for years. She told him it wasn't as bad as he made it out to be. Feeling totally discounted, Frank began to resent Betty, and their relationship deteriorated. It finally broke down several months later when Frank went on strike and stopped cleaning. When Betty came home to a messy house, they got into a terrible fight and Frank moved out. No one was happy. Work had overwhelmed Frank and Betty, and there was not enough communication and empathy to make their day-to-day lives fit with all of the tasks that needed to get done. After receiving counseling, they were able to validate each other's feelings and find other solutions. They divided tasks. Betty traveled less, and Frank promised not to go on any more strikes.

Betty and Frank's case demonstrates a changing trend in our country. Outside work is gaining importance to women. Thirty years ago it was clear that work was the main source of self-esteem for a man, and that women, in general, fed their self-esteem with the quality of their relationships. This has shifted dramatically. Many men have become more relationship-oriented, and many women feel inferior if they do not work outside the home. An article in the *San Francisco Chronicle* in the summer of 1993 reported that women who stay at home with their children are at the greatest risk for depression. The Donna Reed generation is but a longed-for fantasy. The majority of women want to work outside of the home and be recognized for their efforts. On the whole, men ages thirty-five to fifty, raised and programmed in the Donna Reed generation, still unconsciously expect that women will be the primary caretaker of the home and children.

It is hard for them, on an unconscious level, to share the home tasks, even though if asked they will say that they want to be equal partners with their mate. Making the issue of work conscious and bringing it out in the open will help resolve any work-related problems that will arise.

UNCONSCIOUS "WORK PROGRAMMING"

The emotional roots of work from childhood have a powerful hold over us as adults whether we want them to or not. My father's work habits as the owner of a chain of grocery stores left me with the message that men work "all the time." When I was a child and a teenager, I didn't think that fathers should work all the time. They should go to their son's little league games, throw the ball around with them, or read them stories. As I stated in Chapter Eight, I remember telling myself that I would be a different kind of father. Even though my conscious mind wants to be different, my subconscious programming is that men work all the time. When I don't stay focused on what is important to me, I work. I must focus on this every day, because at the end of my life, work will not be nearly as important to me as my relationships with my wife and children. Many, many people, however, never ask themselves what is important to them, and they end up living out the unconscious programming from their childhood. This book is designed to help you reprogram those negative patterns learned in childhood.

My attitude toward yard work as a child also had significant impact on my adult actions. When I was growing up in the San Fernando Valley north of Los Angeles, my family had a mini-ranch with many fruit trees and my father's special dichondra lawn. From my earliest recollections, my brother and I had the task of weeding my father's special dichondra lawn, digging water trenches around the fruit trees, raking leaves and dead fruit, and spraying the weeds in the field with oil from hand-held sprayers. I hated the oil's smell and the way it clung to my clothes and skin. I hated the amount of time yard work took from the things I considered important in life—playing baseball, for example. I found yard work repetitive and boring. I vowed that when I grew up, I would make enough money to hire a gardener and avoid such unpleasant work. Since my mid-twenties I have not mowed or weeded a lawn, and I have a wonderful gardener who cares for my yard. This attitude toward yard work caused some problems in my marriage. My wife loved yard work as a child. She liked to be outside and took pleasure in making her yard look beautiful. She didn't understand why I disliked yard work and accused me of having an aristocratic attitude. It took us several years to work this out. I told her that I would rather spend a few more hours at work a month than use up part of my weekend mowing the lawn.

WHAT ARE THE GOALS OF WORK?

For any couple to be successful together, they must negotiate the work aspects of a relationship. The first step in accomplishing this task is to be clear about the goals of work and to keep those goals uppermost in your mind as you go through your day. Here are the goals of work I use:

- keep life running smoothly
- provide material needs and wants
- provide financial security and the best quality of life for my children, my spouse, and myself
- have the time and resources to enjoy those aspects of my life that are most important to me
- provide a sense of meaning and purpose to life
- make a difference in the lives of my family, friends, and fellow man

Do you have work goals as a couple? Do they complement each other? Is your energy as a couple spent on work that really matters to you as a couple? Or do you spend time working on other people's goals?

Do you work as a team? Or are you individuals, working separately, at crossed purposes to each other? Being focused is key to getting what you want. Later in this chapter, I will ask you to do a worksheet on work values and work goals. Give it the time it needs. Clearly stated work values and goals will direct your energy in a positive way. Without clearly stated work values and goals, your life as a couple is likely to drift from one problem to the next.

ARE YOU WORK'S SLAVE OR MASTER?

If you are not focused on the goals of work in a relationship, you risk becoming work's slave rather than its master. Cynthia and Joel wanted the American Dream. They had been married for nine years and had two small children. Both of their fathers were successful contractors, and Cynthia and Joe were accustomed to having a nice home, driving expensive cars, attending great schools, and going out whenever they wanted. Getting married and having children marked a transition for them. When they realized that they could not afford the house, cars, or other things they wanted on their salaries, they decided to work extra hours at their regular jobs and start a small mail order business of their own on the side. As time passed they grew further and further apart. The pace of their lives was so feverish that they forgot to save time for themselves as a couple, and they frequently felt guilty over the little time they gave to their children. Six years later both Cynthia and Joel were successful in their jobs and they had a thriving mail order business. But they hated their lives. In an attempt to save money, they decided not to hire any employees for their small business, nor would they hire help for home. They had only taken two vacations in nine years. Even though their home was beautiful, they had no time to enjoy it. The pace of their lives unravelled dramatically when their children, now teenagers, showed signs of being out of control. One was having trouble in school;

the other had been caught drunk at a friend's house. When Cynthia and Joel studied their lives closely, they realized that they had become slaves to work. Work was destroying their marriage and their family. They decided to change their lives before they completely lost their marriage and their children. They sold their big house and moved to a smaller, less expensive home (still in a nice neighborhood, but not in the most exclusive area in their city). They sold their expensive cars and bought two family cars that were several years old. With the decreased monthly debt load, they hired two employees to help with their small business, and they spent a lot more time together as a couple and as a family. The American Dream, programmed by the success of their fathers, had cost them too much. It was not worth the price of their marriage and their children. What price are you paying for the dreams programmed into your subconscious? Do you hate the pace of your life? Has your relationship become a slave to work, or have you mastered your efforts so that work brings you closer to your desires and needs. Here are ten rules to help you master work in a relationship.

RULES TO MASTER WORK IN A RELATIONSHIP

1. *Have common goals*: For work to be a satisfying part of the relationship, partners must have common goals, both inside and outside the home. Relationships are under their greatest strain when partners are working for different purposes. When one member wants to work overtime to save money for retirement, and the other wants to accumulate goods, a conflict arises. When one partner wants time off, and the other one wants to make this year better than the last financially, a conflict occurs. When one partner wants the house to look nearly perfect, and that goal is way down on the other partner's list of priorities, a conflict is likely to occur. Establishing clear, written goals for the time you spend working at and away from home will help each partner feel a part of a team and enhance cooperation.

2. *Share tasks:* Relationships do best when partners have a sense of mutual effort or sharing. When one person perceives that they are doing more than the other, resentment may set in. The unhappiness may or may not be spoken, but either way it will affect the relationship. What happens in a work situation when one person carries most of the load? Poor morale. The same thing happens at home. Sit down together and write out all of the different tasks each partner does in a day, week, month, and year. Then write out the time each task takes and compare the list. Do this in a cooperative, curious atmosphere rather than a competitive or blaming one ("I do more than you"). You also may find it helpful as a couple to have periodic work meetings to evaluate the time and necessity of the tasks each member performs.

Sharing tasks can be a particularly sticky issue when one member brings home money and the other stays at home to care for the household and the children. In this case, many women who stay home feel guilty asking for help from their husbands even when they work from the time they get up in the morning to the time they go to bed. Look for mutual understanding and sharing in work to make the relationship be as effective as possible.

3. *Delegate what you can:* Delegation is a forgotten concept with many couples. They often burn out because they haven't reached out for help. Help can come from many sources, such as children, computers, and outside sources.

Soliciting help from children can be beneficial to both the adults and children. Depending on their age, children can do many basic tasks that are time-consuming for adults (dishes, laundry, vacuuming, cooking, picking up). The key to ensuring that work is a positive experience for children is good management strategies by the parents. Like a good manager in a business, it is important for parents to take the time to teach the children how they want certain jobs done.

They then need to supervise closely, reward helpful and effective behavior, and discipline unhelpful or ineffective behavior. Children need supervision, and it seems that many parents just expect their child to know what he or she is supposed to do without proper training. A hundred years ago children played more vital roles in their families than they do today, often earning income that helped the family survive. When children participate in caring for their own families, they develop a sense of meaning and belonging. Even though many parents would argue that their children do nothing but fight over helping out at home, that notion is contradicted by a forty-year study done at Harvard that demonstrated that the only thing that correlates with self-esteem in adults is whether or not they worked as children and teenagers. Work is important to self-esteem. Help boost your children's self-esteem by putting them to work.

Computers also have the potential to save you time at home. As with children, initially you must spend time with them to make the investment pay off, but after that initial investment, you may save hundreds of hours. Checkbook balancing, bill paying, word processing, and personal organizers are just some of the programs available that can begin to make your life easier and the workload more manageable.

Outside help also can save you time and even money in a relationship. Cleaning services, day-care centers, and gardening services can free up time for you to do more profitable work or to spend more time together as a couple. This is especially true when both the partners work outside the home.

4. Have joint work sessions, if it is a positive experience: Some couples work together well, and some couples do nothing but fight when they work together. Know which type you are and use it to your advantage. For those couples who are good at working together, use the work as a way to spend time together, to talk, and to gain a feeling of joint accomplishment. Support each other's efforts and recognize more of what you like about each other than what you don't like (it will encourage you to want to work together more often). For those couples who have difficulty working together, try to understand the reasons behind the problems. For some couples it is a control issue (it has to be done his way or he flies off the handle). For others, the individuals simply may work at different paces. If you don't work together well, don't make a big deal out of it. Find other ways to enjoy each other's company.

5. *Obtain needed skills:* Many people who have trouble at work, whether at home or in the office, are skill deficient. These deficiencies may be caused by real problems such as a learning disorder, or they may be based on erroneous assumptions from the past. For example, Roberta refused to balance the checkbook. She said that she was terrible with numbers and she worried that she would mess it up. This frustrated her husband, Phil, who worked long hours outside the home (Roberta stayed home without any children). He did not want the added buden of household responsibilities. Although he balanced the checkbook each month, he did so grudgingly and was angry while he did it. Finally, he asked Roberta to take a class in personal finance that included basic math concepts and checkbook management. To Roberta's surprise, she easily picked up the concepts of banking. In the class, they did an exercise on personal beliefs about money management. She remembered the experience she had with her sixth grade math teacher who frequently belittled Roberta and told her that she had no math sense. Since then, Roberta had believed she couldn't do math. Understanding that her belief was erroneous and obtaining the necessary skills was all it took for Roberta to take over the checkbook. Lack of the proper skills may be the only thing preventing you from working more efficiently or from working together better as a team. What skills do you need? What erroneous beliefs are holding you back? Question the thoughts in your head that tell you that you can't do something. Often you are unaware of the source of the negative thoughts, which may be keeping you from reaching your goals.

6. *Seek to be efficient:* Efficiency often can make the difference between enjoying work as a couple and feeling overwhelmed by it. Prioritize tasks and stay organized. If you thoughtfully plan, set priorities, and organize, you are less likely to feel frustrated and inefficient. Discussing a task before you begin it and outlining the plan of attack will increase your efficiency. Many couples get distracted in the middle of their tasks and end up with many projects started and few finished. Seek to finish tasks before you start new ones. Also, look for new ways to do things. Don't do something the same way just because that is the way it has always been done. Ask others how they accomplish similar tasks and always look for the most efficient ways to do something.

7. *Periodically, step back and look at what you are doing and why you are doing it:* Many couples have trouble working together because they operate at a different pace. Some people prefer to work nonstop until they finish all of their work. Others prefer to take breaks and complete the work at a more leisurely pace. Either way, breaks from work are important. Sometimes when you are in the middle of a project, it is hard to step back to see what is really going on. When you are working with your partner, plan breaks to rest and also to study the overall picture of what you are doing. Burnout does not result from hard work that is performed to reach worthy goals; it comes from hard work performed for uncertain or unimportant goals.

8. *Understand the myth of workaholism:* Some people think that hard work is somehow a bad thing. They even use the word work as a negative term. They call people who work a lot "workaholics," as if it were

some kind of a disease in need of a twelve-step program. In the late seventies, the term Type A personality added to the negative stereotype of people who worked hard to be successful in their lives. Couples often get involved with this kind of labeling when one member works more than the other one. It is important for couples to understand that work is positive. It adds meaning and purpose to our lives, and it gives us a sense of achievement and control over our own destiny. Without work, people may become depressed, lethargic, and have trouble thinking. Work becomes a problem when a person focuses on the wrong goals, or when the goals motivate one member of the partnership and not the other. Don't downplay or criticize the work itself. Instead, try to refocus so that both partners are traveling in the same direction.

Work involves a clear double-standard with respect to professional and Olympic athletes. These men and women epitomize our idea of workaholism. Yet we idealize their efforts. They struggle hard every day for years and years for a chance at a few moments of glory. If they succeed, we praise them; if they don't succeed we applaud the attempt. Why then is it so wrong for a couple to spend long hours working toward common goals? What are your gold medal goals? What do you want to accomplish with the hard work? What is the end point? With balance, work is good.

9. *Frequently check your attitude:* Attitude is extremely important when people work together. It can either enhance the interaction or destroy it. Attitudes in relationships come from your basic outlooks and beliefs about your partner. When you believe that your partner is lazy or he is dumping the work on you, you look for evidence that substantiates that belief, and you are often irritated with him or her. When you believe that your partner is your ally, and that you both want to work together, you look for evidence that supports your assumptions, and you are often glad to be with each other. We act out of our attitudes.

Attitude is contagious. When you spend time with a partner who is negative or one who puts you down, you will notice that your own mood begins to slip. The opposite is also true. Spending time with a positive, uplifting partner will raise your mood and level of enthusiasm. Do your part to keep the right attitude. Develop attitude checkpoints. Find ways to remind yourself during the day to watch how you think. Some of my patients put helpful phrases, such as "attitude is everything," on their rearview mirrors or on the refrigerator.

10. *Balance work and play to prevent burnout:* Balancing work and play is important to the health of a relationship. Working constantly causes partners to drift emotionally and places the relationship at risk. If one or both partners play too much, the day-to-day details or finances of the relationship may be neglected, which will eventually increase the stress and possibly sour the relationship. Burnout occurs when the relationship is unbalanced. Take time to replenish your best resources, yourself and your lover.

WORKSHEET ON: WORK

Instructions: Fill out the following questions in private. Then come together, share your answers, and listen attentively to the other person before you respond to their answers. Take turns going first on each question.

I. Work Values
Before you clearly define your work goals as a couple, it is important to understand the values and unconscious programming each partner has toward work. Answer the following questions.
A. What work roles did your parents perform when you were growing up?
Your mother:
At home?

At an outside job?
Your father:
At home?
At an outside job?

B. What work roles did you have as a child and teen? What work roles did your partner do at home as a child?

C. What do you believe a woman's role to be?
At home?
At an outside job?
What do you believe a man's role to be?
At home?
At an outside job?

D. If you have children, what do you believe the woman's role should be in caring for them? What do you believe the man's role should be in caring for the children?

E. What do you value in work outside of the home? Please rate the following eleven items from 1 to 11 in order of their importance to you.

	You	Your Partner
money	_____	_____
power	_____	_____
prestige	_____	_____
time off	_____	_____
job security	_____	_____
obtain skills	_____	_____
positive environment	_____	_____
being helpful to others	_____	_____
opportunity for advancement	_____	_____
benefits (health, retirement)	_____	_____
opportunity for creativity	_____	_____

F. What do you value in work inside of the home? Please rate the following eleven items from 1 to 11 in order of their importance to you.

	You	Your Partner
cleanliness	_____	_____
organization	_____	_____
shared responsibility	_____	_____
timeliness	_____	_____
household order	_____	_____
laundry (done well, on time)	_____	_____
meals	_____	_____
positive environment	_____	_____
being helpful to others	_____	_____
opportunity for creativity	_____	_____
efficiency	_____	_____

Are you able to go to bed with dishes in the sink? Why? Why not?

II. Current Feelings Toward Work in the Relationship
A. When you think of work, what are your immediate, unedited feelings? Do you feel motivated and focused? Or do you feel frustrated and alone? Take a moment to write out your feelings.
B. Do you feel that you and your partner work well together? If not, why not?
C. Are there conflicts over work? About what issues?

III. Work Mechanics
A. Home Tasks: who does them? (List the initials of the primary person)
        Preparing meals
        Grocery shopping
        Doing the dishes
        Laundry (wash, folding, putting away)
        Taking care of animals (feeding, cleaning)

Gardening
Yard work
Picking up the house
House cleaning (vacuuming, dusting,
    mopping, etc.)
Paperwork

B. What are your current work roles?
    At home?
    At an outside job?
What are your partner's current work roles?
    At home?
    At an outside job?

C. Does each person have an equal say? If not,
    why not?

D. Does each person know the details of the work
    that is done at home and the work each partner
    does away from home? If not, why not?

SHARED WORK FOCUS STATEMENT

In our work, both in and out of the home, we seek
to share the tasks in a fair and equal way that allows
both of us some of the sweat and some of the glory.
We seek to help each other whenever possible and
make the work we do meaningful, useful, and in line
with the major goals we have for our life together.

Chapter 12

Shared Money Focus:
Who and how in the handling of money; being on the same playing field with money

The management (or mismanagement) of money often leads to significant problems in a relationship. This is such a sensitive issue that many people would rather tell you intimate details about their sexual lives than disclose any financial information. Disagreements over finances are frequently listed in the top three complaints among couples I treat (along with parenting conflicts and sexual problems). Two broad issues underlie financial conflict in relationships: emotional issues and practical or educational issues.

MONEY AND EMOTIONAL ISSUES

Unbeknownst to most people, money causes many emotional or psychological conflicts to surface between couples. Here are several common emotional issues involving money:

Money (like sex) is a power issue. If a couple is not careful, money can be used as a weapon of control. It is not uncommon for the primary breadwinner to communicate (overtly or covertly) that he or she has the right to control the money. This causes the other person to feel inferior. This form of financial control usually backfires when the person with the smaller income becomes resentful. At this point, he or she may use sex to retaliate or may attempt to sabotage the financial plan.

Money is a self-worth issue. Many people equate their sense of self-worth with how much money they make. This is especially true with men and is becoming increasingly so with women. Don and Karen's problem over life insurance is an example of how money is connected to self-worth. Don, a family physician, wanted to protect his family in case he became sick or died. He took out a $1 million life insurance policy on himself. When he discussed this with Karen, she felt devalued because Don did not take out any life insurance on her. "Am I not worth anything if I get hurt or die?" she said. Don replied that she was everything to him, but if something happened to her, he would be able to care for the family financially. It took Karen several weeks to believe that her worth as a person was not tied to how much or how little life insurance she had. Karen saw life insurance as an emotional valuation of her worth, while Don saw the practical issues of family protection.

A particularly tricky money issue occurs when the woman in a relationship makes more than the man. Even though many men say it would not bother them if their wives made more money than they did, when it actually occurs unspoken discomfort often arises between the couple. Men are raised (or preprogrammed) to be more competitive than women, and losing to a girl is often seen as one of the most humiliating experiences that can happen to a boy. As boys become men, this grows into an unconscious attitude that may cause tension in a relationship that is not openly recognized.

I have treated a number of couples where the woman made more money than the man. Commonly, this issue created a level of unspoken discomfort between the couple. Bill and Sue were an example of this. A back injury caused Bill to be on long-term disability from work. Bill felt worthless. He saw his wife go off to work every day while he sat home. Even though he valued the extra time he had with his children, he felt uncomfortable. He felt jealous when his wife was promoted. Consciously, he wanted her to do well because he loved her and knew the extra income would help the family. But a part of him was upset because he no longer had the opportunity to be recognized for his work or to celebrate his accomplishments. Bill's internal sense of himself became so bad that he turned to cocaine to make himself feel better. Fortunately, Bill sought therapy shortly after he turned to drugs. Had he continued the cocaine, it is likely that he would have lost his family.

Of course, a man does not have to be injured for a woman to make more money than him. Her skills may be more in demand; she may have more education than he does; or she may be more motivated than he is. When this occurs, it is important for couples to recognize any underlying conflicts and deal with them in a way that supports their relationship positively. For many people self-worth and money go together.

Ownership of the money, both physically and emotionally, is a powerful emotional issue. Many women have told me that if they are not working or make less money than the man, they do not feel that they own the money. "It's his. I'm just here to take care of his things and his kids," is a common complaint. This attitude involves several problems. One, the woman feels devalued and is more likely to become depressed. Another problem with a lack of ownership of money is unconscious sabotage. A person who does not feel that the money is partly his or hers may take little interest in its proper use and may spend it without considering the overall plan for the money. This person may not have the same level of concern for the money as the one who worked to get it.

Name-calling or attaching negative labels when it comes to money causes problems. People sometimes complain that their partner is cheap or overly concerned about money. Usually their partner feels that the other person is a spendthrift or a compulsive buyer. These negative labels prevent the couple from taking a realistic look at the situation. They psychologically lump each other with all cheap people or compulsive spenders they have ever known and are unable to deal with the situation. It is important to avoid labels and to deal with the real issues. In this case, money has a different meaning for each partner. For the person who is perceived as cheap, saving money may mean freedom from having to work for the rest of his life, security for his family, or the independence to have more time for himself or his family. For the person who is perceived as the spendthrift, money may represent a reward for hard work, enjoyment, status, or power. When couples understand what money means to them, they can look for ways to use teamwork and compromise to reach both sets of goals.

Unfortunately, many couples avoid discussing money at all early in a relationship and never develop clear, joint goals. The emotional issues are never raised, yet remain a constant source of turmoil in the relationship. Money issues may be avoided because one or both partners have a negative attitude toward it, or they associate money with greed. Money and financial issues need to be discussed openly in a healthy relationship. When couples develop clear goals and gather good information on these issues, many money and relationship problems can be solved.

MONEY AND PRACTICAL ISSUES

On a practical level, most people acquire little or no formal education in financial management. Because of this lack of standardized training, many couples are uninformed or mismatched in their financial knowledge. This lack of knowledge leads many couples to an inability to work together to manage their money effectively. They may even end up working against each other. Without proper information, couples are likely to make financial mistakes that strain their finances and subsequently strain their relationships. Knowledge is power. Common knowledge and goals are essential for teamwork, especially in the area of finances.

Common areas of "practical" financial problems include:

- misunderstanding actual income levels (before and after taxes)
- disagreement over spending
- day-to-day mismanagement of money, including balancing the checkbook and paying bills
- varying levels of interest, involvement, or expertise
- disagreement over saving and investment strategies

Couples often get into trouble when they don't plan for the tax man. This is especially true for those couples who are self-employed. Getting hit with an unexpected tax bill can cause stress and anger that may spill over to hurt the relationship. Individuals in a relationship also may overestimate the net money they actually have and live above their means. This causes chronic stress whenever they pay the bills. Another problem for those couples who are financially disorganized is they may forget major purchases they made in the recent past and act as if they never spent that amount of money. They seem surprised when the bills come due, and they don't have as much money as they thought they did. It is essential for couples to go over their finances together on a regular basis. Keeping track of net income is essential to managing money effectively as a couple.

When financial priorities and values are not stated clearly in a relationship, spending disagreements are common. Arguments over where the money goes can go on for years. Some people put a priority on savings, some on comfort toys. Others put a priority on their children's activities or education while others want vacation or holiday money. A written plan with balanced goals will go a long way to alleviate these disagreements.

The day-to-day management of money is also a source of turmoil for many couples. Often, one person takes the lead in managing the money, paying the bills, balancing the checkbook, and caring for savings and investments. When things don't go as planned, the other person may accuse them of mismanagement. The person who handles all the day-to-day details may feel overburdened and resentful, especially when they are criticized. It is important to share daily money management tasks. This keeps both people informed about the finances and encourages them to work toward common goals.

As the number of two-adult working families has increased over the past twenty years, I have seen many couples go to separate financial systems. In these systems, both people keep their own checkbooks and pay their own bills. Each person rationalizes that the money he or she makes belongs to him or her. Each person will contribute his or her share to the relationship and keep the rest to use at his or her own discretion. I believe that this separate system often makes a couple less effective financially. Combining their money and developing a clear financial plan is likely to benefit them more. These separate systems probably developed because of differing financial philosophies and no clear direction or agreement on the best ways to utilize their resources.

As with other issues, individual interest or expertise in handling money varies. Many people have no interest in their monetary situation and leave it up to their spouses or partners. Jerry was an example of this. He didn't like societal values or pressures, so he left the financial issues up to his wife Beth while he wrote science fiction novels. She knew a lot about money, but resented his hands-off approach. After fifteen years, Jerry began to take more of an interest in the couple's finances. This made Beth angry. She told Jerry to stay out of her territory. He had abandoned it years ago, she rationalized, and she had things under control. Control was a word that suited Beth. She liked controlling the finances and didn't want Jerry to interfere. To heal this part of their relationship, they both had to change. Beth had to give up some control, and Jerry had to take initiative more regularly. Having a partner one-up or one-down in financial knowledge (or in any part of the relationship) can cause turmoil. Shared knowledge is the best.

Too many couples are unprepared for their future, especially considering predictions that the social security fund will be unavailable to our young people when they are older and that people will live years longer than ever before in history. Many individuals within a relationship do not understand the importance of saving for the future and get into disagreements over how they spend their funds. Having a clear savings and investment strategy is crucial to financial health.

The following plan will help you develop clear financial goals and, based on those goals, give you clear direction on how to use your resources as a couple. This chapter will help each partner be on equal footing when it comes to money knowledge and will offer means of learning to share responsibility and decision making. In addition, I have included several forms that will help the couple quickly organize their finances, allowing each partner immediate information on their financial situation.

WORKSHEET ON: FINANCES

- What are your financial values?
- What are your feelings about finances in this relationship?
- Are there conflicts over money? About what issues?
- What are your financial dreams and goals?
- How much do you make as a couple?
- How much do you spend (and on what)?
- How much do you save?
- How much do you need for retirement?

- Do you have shared checking and savings accounts?
- Who pays what bills?
- Who is the spending authority?
- Who complains about money in your system?
- Who doesn't seem to care much or know much about money?
- Where is the information kept?

These are essential questions to answer if you want to manage your finances effectively. Having clear expectations and shared financial goals can increase the sense of teamwork and mutual support and can significantly decrease the tensions that often surround money issues. As I discussed above, the day-to-day management of the finances can be another source of stress. Establishing clear roles with check-in points gives the couple clear direction and helps put each partner on equal footing when it comes to the financial health of the household.

INSTRUCTIONS:

Fill out the following questions in private. If you do not have all of the income figures, estimate them. It will be interesting for you to see how closely your beliefs match reality. Then meet with your partner, share your answers; and listen attentively to the other person before you respond to their answers. Take turns going first on each question.

I. *What Are Your Financial Values?*
Rank the uses for your money in the order of their importance to you (1 = most important, 12 = least important).

___Maintain or expand current lifestyle (housing, transportation)

___Security, present (savings account)

___Security, future (retirement, life insurance)

___ Risk taking/investment money

___ Fun/Pleasure, present (concerts, plays, sporting events, hobbies)

___ Fun/Pleasure, future (vacations, hobbies)

___ Material goods (television, clothes, adult toys)

___ Children's education, present and future

___ Future education for adults

___ Prestige items (buying things so that others will think you are successful)

___ Giving to charities and important personal causes

___ Pets

To increase your success in managing your finances as a couple, the joint decisions you make about money need to be based on mutual financial values. Look for areas of compatibility and compromise.

II. What are the current financial feelings in the relationship?

A. When you think of money and finances, what are your immediate, unedited feelings? Are you relaxed and focused, or are you frustrated and panicky? Take a moment to write out your feelings.

B. Write out your opinion on why you feel the way you do.

III. Are there conflicts over money? About what are the issues?

IV. What are the mechanics of your financial system?

A. Who handles the day-to-day finances? Are the financial tasks/chores shared? If not, why not?

B. Does each person have an equal say? If not, why not?

C. Does each person know the financial details of the resources and expenditures? If not, why not?

D. Is anyone left in the dark? If yes, why?

For you to have a clear picture of your finances as a couple, you must know your net income (after taxes), expenses, and net worth.

V. *What is your net income* (estimate if not known, go back later together and fill out more accurate information)?

A. Where does your money come from (before taxes)? List sources and amount per month and year.

	Month	Year
Employment/Partner #1:	____	____
(Salaries, tips, commissions, and bonuses)		
Employment/Partner #2	____	____
(Salaries, tips, commissions, and bonuses)		
Interest income:	____	____
Current investment income:	____	____
(dividends, stocks, bonds)		
Retirement income (if at retirement age):	____	____
(IRAs, pensions, annuities)		
Real estate income:	____	____
Inheritance (current and potential):	____	____
Money gifts:	____	____
Income tax refunds:	____	____
Other:	____	____
Other:	____	____
Other:	____	____
Average gross income before taxes?	____	____

B. What is your tax burden?

	Month	Year
Federal taxes (estimate):	____	____
State taxes (estimate):	____	____
Local taxes (estimate):	____	____
FICA (estimate):	____	____

Estimate withholdings: This can be done by looking at your pay stub or, if you do not get a pay stub each month, go through the following simple procedures. To estimate your federal withholding tax, look at your gross yearly income and refer to last year's tax tables. Do the same for state and local taxes. Record these figures above. If you pay FICA, figure an estimate by multiplying 7.65 percent of the first $53,400 of your income (1992 laws). If you are self-employed, you pay 15.3 percent.

C. What is your net yearly income?

Figure your net yearly income by subtracting your total tax burden a year from your gross income. Then divide it by 12 to get your net monthly income.

Average total income a month after taxes?

Average total income a year after taxes?

*VI. **What are your expenses** (estimate if not known, go back later together and fill out more accurate information)?*

How is your money being spent currently, on a monthly and yearly basis? If you do not know, estimate and then later on find out. This will tell you if your spending habits fit with your values.

	Month	Year
HOUSEHOLD		
mortgage/rent:	_____	_____
(include principal, interest, taxes, and insurance)		
condo/homeowners dues:		
parking:	_____	_____
utilities:	_____	_____
(heat, gas, electricity, water, trash)		
telephone:		
cable television:	_____	_____
repairs:	_____	_____
maid service:	_____	_____
SUB TOTAL	_____	_____

	Month	Year

TRANSPORTATION
gas: _____ _____
upkeep/repairs: _____ _____
public transportation: _____ _____
SUBTOTAL   _____ _____

FOOD
groceries: _____ _____
(including food, paper products, and toiletries)
meals away from home: _____ _____
SUBTOTAL   _____ _____

CLOTHING/SELF CARE
new clothes: _____ _____
new shoes: _____ _____
laundry: _____ _____
clothes or shoe repair: _____ _____
hair stylist/barber: _____ _____
other: _____ _____
other: _____ _____
SUBTOTAL   _____ _____

MEDICAL
doctor: _____ _____
(not covered by insurance or deductible)
dentist: _____ _____
(not covered by insurance or deductible)
medications: _____ _____
SUBTOTAL   _____ _____

PROTECTION
life insurance: _____ _____
health insurance: _____ _____
dental insurance: _____ _____
auto insurance: _____ _____
disability insurance: _____ _____
umbrella insurance: _____ _____
SUBTOTAL   _____ _____

	Month	Year

SAVINGS/INVESTMENTS
emergency fund:
holiday fund:
retirement fund:
(IRA/SEP/KEOGH, pension, annuity,
whole/universal life cash value)
investments:
SUBTOTAL

DEBTS/INSTALLMENTS
auto loan:
student loans:
credit cards:
other:
other:
SUBTOTAL

EMPLOYMENT-RELATED EXPENSES
child care:
organization dues:
publications:
equipment:
SUBTOTAL

EDUCATION/LESSONS
adult:
(include tuition, books, fees)
children:
(include tuition, books, fees)
SUBTOTAL

ENTERTAINMENT/RECREATION/GIFTS
fun/pleasure, present:
(concerts, plays, sporting events, hobbies)
fun/pleasure, future:
(vacations, hobbies)
gifts:
SUBTOTAL

	Month	Year
PERSONAL IMPROVEMENT AND COMMUNITY		
health clubs:	_____	____
service clubs:	_____	____
church:	_____	____
charity:	_____	____
SUBTOTAL	_____	____
PETS		
food:	_____	____
health:	_____	____
supplies:	_____	____
SUBTOTAL	_____	____
OTHER		
child support:	_____	____
alimony:	_____	____
legal expenses:	_____	____
SUBTOTAL	_____	____
Average total fixed expenses?	_____	____

VII. What are your total excess finances versus total short finances?

Net Monthly Income_____ minus
Net Monthly Expenses (_____) equals
Total Excess (Short) Monthly Monies_____

Net Yearly Income _____ minus Net
Yearly Expenses (_____) equals
Total Excess (Short) Yearly Monies_____

VIII. What Is Your Net Worth? (Estimate if not known; go back later together and fill out more accurate information.)

A. Assets
    CASH
        savings accounts: _____
        checking accounts: _____
        credit union accounts: _____
        insurance cash value: _____
    SECURITIES
        U.S. bonds: _____
        other bonds: _____
        stocks (current market value):   _____
        CDs: _____
        notes and loans due: _____
    REAL ESTATE (market value)
        #1:   _____
        #2:   _____
    RETIREMENT ACCOUNTS
        IRA/SEP/KEOGHs: _____
        annuity value: _____
    OTHER PROPERTY (market value)
        automobiles: _____
        jewelry: _____
        collections: _____
        furniture: _____
        equipment: _____
        tools: _____
        Total Assets: _____

B. Liabilities
    CURRENT LIABILITIES
        mortgage: _____
        other real estate loans: _____
        automobile loans: _____
        student loans: _____
        medical debts: _____
        legal debts: _____
        bank loans: _____
        credit cards: _____
        back taxes: _____
        other: _____
        Total Liabilities: _____

Total Assets_____ minus Total Liabilities
(_____) equals Net Worth

IX. Consistency Factor

After you examine your financial values, income, and outflow, how do your spending patterns seem to fit with your values about money?

A. Financial Goals

Given what you know now about your financial values, income, outflow, and net worth, what are your goals and dreams that relate to your monetary resources? What is really important to you?

- Do you have current written financial goals as a couple?
- If yes, list them in order of priority.
- Specific Goal Areas: Write out your goal for each area in one-year, five-year, and ten-year increments.

COUPLE INCOME LEVEL
One Year: _____
Five Year: _____
Ten Year: _____

HOUSING
One Year: _____
Five Year: _____
Ten Year: _____

VALUE OF SAVINGS ACCOUNTS
One Year: _____
Five Year: _____
Ten Year: _____

VALUE OF RETIREMENT ACCOUNTS
One Year: _____
Five Year: _____
Ten Year: _____

VALUE OF EDUCATIONAL ACCOUNTS FOR CHILDREN
    One Year: _____
    Five Year: _____
    Ten Year: _____

AUTOMOBILES
    One Year: _____
    Five Year: _____
    Ten Year: _____

OTHER MATERIAL ITEMS (equipment, boats, televisions, stereos)
    One Year: _____
    Five Year: _____
    Ten Year: _____

VACATIONS/TRAVEL
    One Year: _____
    Five Year: _____
    Ten Year: _____

CHARITY/GIVING
    One Year: _____
    Five Year: _____
    Ten Year: _____

NET WORTH
    One Year: _____
    Five Year: _____
    Ten Year: _____

B. What Kind of Financial Lifestyle Do You Want?
Living from paycheck to paycheck? Or working toward mutual goals that excite both partners?

Don't be a victim of your spending habits. Instead ensure that your spending behavior fits with the goals you have as a couple for your monetary resources.

XI. *Financial information summary form*
Checking Account numbers and Balances:

_____

Checking Account Numbers and Balances:

_____

Checking Account Numbers and Balances:

_____

Saving Account Numbers and Balances:

_____

Saving Account Numbers and Balances:

_____

Saving Account Numbers and Balances:

_____

IRA Account Numbers and Balances:

_____

IRA Account Numbers and Balances:

_____

SEP-IRA Account Numbers and Balances:

_____

KEOGH Account Numbers and Balances:

_____

Pension Account Numbers and Balance:

_____

Pension Account Numbers and Balance:

_____

Stock/Bond Account Numbers and Balance:

_____

Stock/Bond Account Numbers and Balance:

_____

Stock/Bond Account Numbers and Balance:

_____

Loan Account Numbers and Balances:

_____

Mortgage Loan Account Numbers and Balances:

_____

Mortgage Loan Account Numbers and Balances:

_____

Home Equity Loan Account Numbers and Balances:

_____

Automobile Loan Account Numbers and Balances:
_____

Automobile Loan Account Numbers and Balances:
_____

Student Loan Account Numbers and Balances:
_____

Student Loan Account Numbers and Balances:
_____

Personal Loans (when, to whom, and balance):
_____

Personal debts (when, to whom, and balance):
_____

Last Will and Testament (where kept? executor?):
_____

Birth Certificates (address of hospital or county office where kept):
_____

Insurance Agent (name and address):
_____

Stockbroker (name and address):
_____

Additional Resources:

Quicken (computer programs)
Wealth Without Risk, Charles Givens
More Wealth Without Risk, Charles Givens
The Business of Living, Stephen M. Pollan and
    Mark Levine
The Budget Kit, Judy Lawrence
Bonnie's Household Budget Book, Bonnie Runyan
    McCullough
Cure Your Money Ills, Michael Slavit

SHARED MONEY FOCUS STATEMENT

Money and finances are issues we share and talk about. We both choose to be in the know about our money. Sound money management is essential to the overall health of our relationship. We share with each other thoughts on the best ways to obtain and save money. We spend our resources in a way consistent with our short-term and long-term goals. We balance frugality with the ability to spend our resources on fun and pleasure.

Chapter 13

Shared Personal Focus:

Meaning and purpose, intellectual growth, spiritual health, emotional health, physical health

In any relationship it is important not to lose your individuality, not to lose yourself as a unique person. Relationships often get into the most trouble when you become dependent upon your partner to meet all of your emotional needs. To that end, it is necessary for each person in a relationship to develop his or her own, individual goals. This chapter will help you as an individual within a relationship develop a personal focus statement. Goals that, for the most part, affect you directly. By developing these goals, you will add an even sharper focus to your life. You also will be able to share them with your partner so that he or she can support and encourage you.

Many people who have come to me for help have lost themselves in relationships that ended up failing. When the relationship was over, these people felt so abandoned, lost, and alone that they didn't know where to turn. During my psychiatric training, I treated a woman named Lenore. She was admitted to the hospital after she tried to kill herself by putting her head inside a gas oven. Her husband had just left her, and she felt that her whole world had unravelled. She had devoted herself to him. She helped put him through school. She cared for the children while he worked long hours. She cooked, cleaned, did the laundry, and made love to him when he was in the mood. She had no life outside of him and the children. She had no idea who she was supposed to be. She was scared. Because she had spent her life as a homemaker, she believed that she had no marketable skills for the workplace. She felt hopeless, thus the suicide attempt. Initially, the therapy was difficult. She had trouble finding herself without her husband. Every time she thought of him and her broken life, she cried. We reached a turning point when I asked her to describe her life before she met her husband. Before they met in college, Lenore considered herself a competent person. She was an honor roll student, she had many friends, and she always received outstanding evaluations at work. She had worked part-time in a travel agency where she had been promoted because of her ability to learn complicated material quickly. When she rediscovered her competent self, she began to heal. Her suicidal thoughts were the first to go. Next she got a job in a travel agency. Two years later she applied for and received a small business loan and started her own travel agency, which turned out to be quite successful. As I predicted to her, the stronger she grew emotionally, the more her husband started to show interest in her. She was too hurt to have anything to do with him, but it made her feel good to be able to be the one to say she wasn't interested anymore. In fact, three years after her suicide attempt she sent her ex-husband a thank you card for leaving her. In it she wrote, "By leaving me you helped me find myself. Somehow when we were married, I lost who I was. Now I'm found, and it feels good. —Lenore"

Pat's situation resembled Lenore's. He had trouble finding himself in his wife's shadow. His wife was a successful singer. She traveled around the world; she was loved by her fans; and she made enough money so that both she and Pat would never have to work again. Although Pat was happy that his wife enjoyed success, he lived in her shadow. He couldn't shake the idea of her success. He felt unimportant, worthless. He often thought of leaving, but he loved his wife. Deep down he knew that it was his problem and he sought help through therapy. One of my first questions to Pat was, "What's important to you? What do you want for your life?" The question surprised him. Although his identity was the central issue, he had never taken the time to ask himself, "What's important to me?" He was too busy being jealous and feeling unimportant. He then began to see his wife's success as an asset rather than a liability. It gave him the opportunity to work on charity projects in his community. He headed up a local shelter for homeless families and took a particular interest in homeless children. After doing this for several years he became recognized as an expert statewide.

It doesn't have to take separations, divorce, or suicide for you to find out who you are as a person separate from your partner. It takes personal seeking, planning, and goal setting. What do you want for yourself, all by yourself? Take time to answer the following questions.

- What kind of difference do you want to make with your life?
- Where do you find meaning and purpose in your life?
- Will the world be a better place because of your existence?
- Are you learning new things?
- Are you challenged and stimulated by the world around you?
- Or, are you bored and waiting to retire or take a cruise?
- How do you feel emotionally?
- Does your emotional state help you or hurt you?
- How do you perceive God? Helpful, interested in your life, indifferent, or not there at all?
- Do you have spiritual goals?
- What are your beliefs about the meaning of life and death?
- Do you believe in a hereafter, in a heaven or hell?

- What do you want your body to look like?
- What are your health goals?
- How long do you want to live?

These are the questions we will explore in this chapter to help you develop your own personal focus statement.

MEANING AND PURPOSE

What kind of difference do you want to make with your life? Where do you find meaning and purpose in your life? Will the world be a better place because of your existence? Meaning, purpose, and making a difference are essential to a fulfilled life. Most people pass their days dealing with the problems and challenges in their lives without asking themselves why they do what they do. What does your life mean? Why do you breathe, eat, sleep, work, make love, and relate? What is your life for? These are weighty questions, but when you answer them, they will change your existence. They changed Paul's.

At age thirty-one Paul was diagnosed with testicular cancer. Up until then he had been a real go-getter. He had his MBA and he had been working at his company for three years. His goal was to be a vice-president in five years and he was almost there. He worked nights and weekends; his free time was filled with schmoozing (working dinners and work-related golf games). He constantly thought about being successful at work. At first when he found the lump in his testicle, he didn't think much of it. "I'm only thirty-one years old," he thought, "nothing is the matter with me." But when it continued to grow, he got scared and sought help. The cancer diagnosis frightened him. He had never known anyone who had cancer so young. He had never even thought about dying. He was forced to confront his mortality head on. The doctor told him that this kind of cancer is potentially curable, but it would involve surgery and chemotherapy. In an instant, all of Paul's work, all of the long hours, meant nothing to him. He didn't care about becoming a vice president, and he didn't care about schmoozing or "massaging his image." He cared about life itself. He cared about his loved ones. All he wanted to do was spend time with his wife and his two little girls. He had so much to teach his children, he couldn't let the cancer cheat them out of a father. Paul discovered true meaning in his relationship with his family. Through surgery, chemotherapy, and love, Paul was cured of his cancer. After three years, all signs of it vanished. Paul still worked for the same company, but at a much more relaxed pace. If he made vice-president, that was great; but he was unwilling to let his job run his life. He ran it. He stopped working nights and weekends; he became actively involved in his church which is something he had been meaning to do; and he spent a lot of time with his wife and girls. Paul found the true meaning of life by facing his own death. He wanted to make a difference in his daughters' lives, and he tried to make the world a better place through his work at home and in his church.

Are you the kind of person who needs a tragedy to change your life? Or are you often in the process of seeking and evaluating your goals and motivation? Make your life count at home, at work, with others, and within yourself.

Ask yourself, "What do I need from my partner to make my life have more meaning and purpose?" Communicate your needs to your partner.

FOCUS STATEMENT FOR MEANING AND PURPOSE

I am growing as an individual and making a difference in the lives of others whenever I can.

INTELLECTUAL STIMULATION AND THE DANGERS OF BELIEVING YOUR OWN BALONEY

Are you learning new things? Are you challenged and stimulated by the world around you? Or, are you bored and waiting to retire or to take a cruise? Many people think of learning as a childhood, teenage, or young adult activity. They look forward to the days when they don't have to study anymore, when they know what they need to know. This view of learning, however, causes people to grow old. Learning is certainly one of the fountains of youth.

Dr. Marian Diamond, professor of anatomy at the University of California, Berkeley, reported ground-breaking research on the brain in her book *Enriching Heredity*. She demonstrated the need for people to continue to learn actively throughout the life cycle. Her research suggested that a person's brain begins to deteriorate when they do not actively use their mind. People who retire and just "putter," along with people who live in rest homes that provide little stimulation, find that their ability to think, concentrate, and remember significantly weakens. On the other hand, older people who are actively engaged in learning new things and sharing ideas have sharper mind skills. She gave the example of a ninety-eight-year-old university chemist who was still active in writing and research. Growing older does not cause a deterioration in function, Dr. Diamond postulates. A lack of use is the problem. In many ways your brain is like a muscle; the more you use it the stronger it becomes. The less you use it the more it wastes away. The phrase "use it or lose it" applies to your brain. Working and stimulating your brain keeps it young.

Albert Einstein once said that if you study anything for fifteen minutes a day, you will be an expert in that field within a year. If you study something for fifteen minutes a day for five years you will be a national expert. Fifteen minutes a day is not much time to devote yourself to be a national expert. What interests you? What turns you on? What do you want to be an expert in? It is essential to have your own intellectual pursuits to keep your mind in top physical and emotional condition.

At the age of forty-seven, my friend Gail wanted to go to nursing school. From a monetary standpoint she didn't need to work. Her husband had a comfortable salary and he wanted her to stay at home to be with him. She felt the need to have her own accomplishments and her own intellectual pursuits. Initially, her husband felt threatened. He feared he would lose her if she ventured into the work world. I told him that he might lose her if he kept her from reaching her goals and dreams. Gail loved school. She loved the challenge of learning new things, and she loved learning to help other people through nursing. After a year of nursing school, she told me that her mind was as sharp as when she was twenty years old.

Men often try to keep their wives from developing their own intellectual interests, somehow feeling threatened by their independence. It is a mistake to hold them back, because when you prevent people from pursuing their interests, their resentment builds and they withdraw from you emotionally. Henry refused to allow his wife Cathy to go back to school. She said that the kids were all in school, and she wanted to keep her mind engaged in interesting pursuits. Henry said that school was a waste of time and money and he wouldn't allow it. Because she didn't want to make waves, Cathy relinquished the idea of school. Instead, she began having an affair to occupy her time. I have heard several stories like Cathy's. Seek ways to help your partner obtain the stimulation their mind needs so that they don't look elsewhere for stimulation.

Ted Shapiro, M.D., chairman of child psychiatry at Columbia University in New York, spent a week with me as a visiting professor during my psychiatric training. He told me, "Everyone believes their own baloney." He went on to say that the essence of learning is having a critical mind that is able to question. He said, "Believing something just because you always have is the biggest roadblock to personal or intellectual growth." Think of how toddlers learn: they ask many questions (often to their parents' dismay), and they are continually curious about their world. Curiosity and questioning are healthy developmental signs for toddlers. Unfortunately for many adults, as we begin to "believe our own baloney," curiosity, questioning, and learning begin to vanish.

Here are four important keys to learning and intellectual stimulation. I teach my patients these principles, because using them makes real change possible.

Be curious. It is the ultimate form of being alive and human. Curiosity is the basis for any learning and keeps you looking for answers in an interested, reflective way. I am often concerned by the lack of curiosity in many teenagers and adults. Without curiosity no real learning can occur. Curiosity is especially helpful to people who are in the middle of a panic attack. If they can be curious about what started it, what is happening in their body, and what they are thinking about while it occurs, their chances of breaking the attack dramatically increase.

Ask lots of questions. Formulating the right questions is critical to finding answers. Many people shy away from asking important questions because they are embarrassed, worried about what others think of them, and/or think they should already know the answer. Don't be held back by these thoughts. They are not useful. One of the reasons toddlers ask why so much is that they don't understand and they want to. We need to follow their example and ask why until we understand. Always be a student, even when you are teaching. You already know your stuff. Why not get the best of what someone else has to offer?

Be observant. Watch yourself and others as you go through your day. Especially keep tabs on the thoughts that go through your head and how you react to others. Real learning comes from observing the world around you.

Think critically. Don't believe something just

because someone else said it to you. Look for evidence that makes sense to you. And keep asking why until you understand. Your attitude toward life determines how much you learn. I like the phrase, "When the student is ready, the teacher will appear."

Scientific inquiry is based on these principles. Many people would be surprised to know that they are also essential to psychotherapy. If you can be curious about yourself, ask lots of questions, observe your life as you go through it, and think critically, you have a chance at getting what you want out of life and being healthy in the process.

Ask yourself, "What do I need from my partner to make my life more intellectually stimulating." Communicate that need to your partner.

FOCUS STATEMENT ON INTELLECTUAL STIMULATION

I actively seek to stimulate my brain by learning new information. I also seek a give-and-take with others for the mutual benefit of gaining and giving information, allowing for the possibility of new ideas in my life.

EMOTIONAL HEALTH

How do you feel emotionally? Does your emotional state help you or hurt you? These questions are critical to a healthy relationship. Before you can engage in a healthy relationship you must first have a healthy sense of yourself. How you feel about yourself often determines how you feel about others and the world around you.

Richard Gardner, M.D., a prominent psychiatrist, once said, "The meaning of life is that the world is a Rorschach Test. You get what you expect you'll get." The Rorschach Test is the famous ink blot test. A tester holds up ink blots and the subject tells the tester what he or she sees in the ink blots. By themselves, the ink blots mean nothing. It is what the person sees in them that reveals information about the person. If the person feels good inside, he or she is likely to see healthy images. When the person feels sad, nervous, or mad inside, he or she is likely to see depressing, anxiety-provoking, or hostile images in the ink blots. You see the world through the filters of your mind. Therefore, it is important to clean the filters of your mind regularly.

GETTING AND STAYING BETTER

The joy of my work as a psychiatrist is to watch individuals and couples heal. Sometimes it happens quickly, sometimes it happens over longer periods of time. As I have helped and watched my patients heal over the years, I have noticed eight common elements connected to getting and staying better. These elements can help anyone at any stage of life, and they are essential to your emotional health.

1. Be responsible for yourself, not a victim of someone else's behavior. Taking responsibility for your actions is the foundation for mental health. Whenever you blame someone else for the problems in your life, you become powerless to change anything. Taking responsibility for your life gives you the power to control what happens to you and also to change the things you don't like about your life. I recently told a stress group I teach, "You're not fat, hypertensive, anxious, or depressed because of how your children, husband, or job treat you; you're fat, hypertensive, anxious, or depressed because of how you react to how they treat you." You are responsible for how you interact with the world. Not anyone else.

2. Focus on your goals. Many people go through life never knowing what they really want out of life. As a result, they go from crisis to crisis without directing their energy toward goals that are important to them. In each situation you face, ask yourself what your goal is and what you can do to reach it. It is amazing how many opportunities you will see if you can define clearly what you want out of life.

3. *Treat yourself as a good mother would.* Be firm and kind to yourself, and notice and nurture the child inside you. How you treat yourself is critical to how you treat others. If you are self-critical, then odds are you are also critical of others. A good mother is someone who is firm with her child and makes him or her do the things that are good for the child. She also always recognizes more good than bad in the child and is her child's best cheerleader.

4. *Pay attention to how you think.* How you think moment by moment has a tremendous impact on how you feel. If you tend to think negatively or to predict the worst, then you are likely to have problems with depression or nervousness. Talk back to the a.n.t.s and "critic's committee" in your head, and replace negative thoughts with positive, hopeful images that spur you on to believe you can do anything you set your mind to do.

5. *Refuse ever to let anyone treat you in an abusive way.* Basically, I think we teach other people how to treat us. If we stand up for ourselves, people are more likely to treat us with respect. If we are overly subservient to others, then many people will treat us like doormats. Your emotional stance toward yourself is the biggest indicator of how others will deal with you.

6. *Remember that your feelings can lie to you.* Feelings come from complex memories and hurts from the past mixed with what is happening in the present. When you have strong negative feelings, it is important to check them out against the facts before believing them. For example, if you feel as though your spouse doesn't love you, ask yourself what concrete evidence you have for feeling that way. Many people misread situations when they are feeling down on themselves, and they project these feelings onto others. Check out strong feelings before you believe them.

7. Consider the mistakes you make as valuable learning experiences. Being able to learn from your mistakes is critical to psychological growth. When I see new patients, I tell them that through the course of psychotherapy, they will have down times and that it is essential for us to learn about them and to recognize them as important experiences. If we can understand the dips, I explain, then we can prevent them in the future.

8. Have the ability to be present in and conscious about your life. Patterns from the past do not have to haunt you or control you. I have come to believe that a great many people live their lives in an unconscious state, never really deciding what is important or directing their lives in a way that makes them proud. Live in the present and focus your energy on achieving the goals you have set for yourself.

Getting and staying better is a never-ending process that requires us to be aware of who we are and what we are doing here on this earth. Challenge yourself to be a positive, life-giving force to yourself and those around you.

DEALING WITH STRESS

How you handle stress in your life also plays a huge role in your emotional health. Stress is part of all of our lives. It comes at us from many sides. When we handle stress ineffectively, it can destroy our physical and emotional lives; when we handle it constructively, it enhances our sense of competence and well-being.

The three most common sources of stress are the environment, our bodies, and our thoughts. Environmental stress includes such things as the weather, crowds, noise, freeways, relationships, time pressure, and work. Physical stress is brought on by illness, accidents, hormonal changes (adolescence, menstrual cycle, and menopause), aging, and poor eating or sleeping habits. The way we think also can be a source of tremendous stress. Guilt, anger, depression, negative thoughts, predicting the worst, and reliving past traumatic events all contribute to the stress we feel.

Here are lists of ten ineffective ways to cope with stress and ten helpful ideas for handling stress:

INEFFECTIVE COPING

1. Alcohol and drugs: This is a very common way to handle stress. Alcohol and drugs, however, are only temporary solutions and actually work against fighting stress. They work by prematurely releasing natural mood chemicals, thus depleting your reserves.

2. Overeating: this is another common approach to stress which, like alcohol or drugs, makes you feel better for the moment, but worse in the long run.

3. Make things out to be worse than they really are: negative thoughts are fuel for stress. Whenever we predict the worst or become gloomy and pessimistic, we drain our emotional energy and feel like hiding out.

4. Social isolation: many people withdraw from others during times of stress. This takes us away from potential sources of help, leaving us too much time to brood.

5. Procrastination: the more you put things off the more you have to do. This often overwhelms the stressed-out person, making things worse.

6. Blame: making someone else responsible for your problems. This victim posture is extremely dangerous because it steals away your ability to control stress.

7. Avoid conflict: many people are conflict phobic, and are afraid of rational confrontations with the people who may be contributing to their stress. Keeping the anger inside and allowing it to build up often contributes to depression and anxiety problems.

8. Too much television, or lack of brain exercise: many people "veg out" when they are stressed. Unfortunately, the less you work your brain the weaker it becomes. Many people complain of poor concentration and memory if they have let their minds go dormant for any prolonged period.

9. Lack of focus: you forget what is really important in your life. Stress often causes people to lose sight of their major goals. This prevents them from achieving any personal or professional growth. This is seen in people who are always trying to help others at the expense of themselves.

10. Excessive anger: this occurs when you dump on the important people in your life, alienating your support system. This occurs frequently. For example, if a man is having trouble at work and becomes overly critical at home, he alienates his family at a time when he needs them most.

HELPFUL COPING

1. Clear focus: focus your thoughts and behavior toward what you really want out of your life.

2. Take responsibility for things you can change and let go of the things you can't change. Stay away from blaming others for what is going wrong in your life.

3. Positive thoughts: you can choose the thoughts you focus on. Choose happy, optimistic, and hopeful thoughts. It will make a major change in your attitude.

4. Spend time around positive people. Choose to spend your time with people who support and uplift you.

5. Getting work done and out of your brain. Beat procrastination by focusing on completing projects. You'll feel so much better.

6. Sensible eating: what you eat plays an important role in how you feel. Choose to eat foods that are healthy for you.

7. Deal with conflict in a positive, constructive way.

Assert yourself in a positive way. Be kind if possible and be a good listener.

8. Engage in interesting activities that stimulate your mind.

9. Physical exercise is often an effective way to work off excessive anxiety and to lift a depression.

10. Spend time each day doing some form of mental relaxation.

This can take the form of performing slow deep-breathing exercises, visualizing a relaxing place, or meditating. Prayer is often a wonderful tool for relieving stress.

Your emotional health matters, keep it in top shape. Ask yourself, "What do I need from my partner to help my emotional life be as healthy as possible?" Communicate it to your partner.

FOCUS STATEMENT ON EMOTIONAL HEALTH

I encourage myself to be responsible, positive, focused, thoughtful, and to learn from my mistakes. I am a good parent to myself, praising successful attitudes in myself and constructively correcting attitudes that hold me back.

SPIRITUAL HEALTH

How do you perceive God? Helpful, interested in your life, indifferent, absent? Do you have spiritual goals? Spiritual guidelines? What are your beliefs about the meaning of life and death? Do you believe in a hereafter? In a heaven or hell?

Many books on relationships totally leave out the notion of God. Yet, clearly 70 percent of the population in the United States claim to have a sincere belief in God and actively participate in some form of worship. Spiritual needs and values play an important role in human behavior whether we admit this to ourselves or not. Your spiritual outlook affects how you interact with the world day-to-day. If you believe in a judgment day, you are more likely to be cognizant of your behavior. If you believe God is watching and criticizing your every move, you are likely to be self-critical. If you believe that God is kind and forgiving, you are likely to be kind and forgiving to yourself and others. If you believe God is present in your life, you are likely to use prayer to help your life be more effective. If you believe that God is an abstract idea, you are likely to experience an existential feeling of isolation and loneliness. Spirituality and spiritual beliefs play a powerful role in everyday life.

How you see the face of God in your life often determines your behavior. Peggy and Ron had been active in their church during the fifteen years of their marriage. They raised their children in the faith; they prayed together; and they taught a Bible study together. Like most people their lives were filled with good times and bad times. The good times included having their children, buying their dream home, being active in a church they loved, and vacations. The bad times, although less frequent, did not strain their faith (two miscarriages, a robbery, and a job layoff). Their faith helped them through the rough spots. This was true even when Ron was diagnosed with terminal cancer at the age of fifty-three. Many people would have been bitter and may have turned away from their faith, but again Ron and Peggy were thankful for their life and used their faith in God and an afterlife to fuel a sense of inner peace.

In my practice, I see many people who question the very existence and character of God. They ask questions such as, If God is good, why is there so much evil in the world? If God cares, why do children get cancer? If God is real, he must be cruel to allow the suffering. How can I believe in a God I cannot see? These are hard questions to answer. But for me, when I look up at the stars at night, look at a wave gently crashing on the sand, or look into the faces of my sleeping children, I detect a magnificent order that is beyond the random chaos of a godless evolution. I often think of the second law of physics, "entropy," which says that matter in the universe goes from order to disorder, or from order to chaos. In looking at the beauty of the world, especially on a moonlit night, one can see order.

The purpose of this section of the book is not to encourage you to believe or not to believe in God, but for you to clarify what you believe and then to ask yourself, "Does my behavior fit the spiritual goals I have set for my life?" If your behavior fits your spiritual goals, you will have an internal sense of integrity. If your behavior does not match your spiritual goals, you will have an inner sense of unrest and turmoil. If you are conscious of the spiritual guidelines that direct your life, you will be focused and centered. I often share the New Testament verse "Love your neighbor as yourself" as a helpful guideline for my patients. To me this verse means that to be loving toward others, you must first be loving toward yourself. Love for others flows from your feelings within. Loving yourself and others is essential to spiritual health.

One way to evaluate your own spirituality is to look at your prayer life. Whether you admit it or not, we all pray. We all have our own way of talking with God or conversing with the universe. Some people communicate with God in a ritualized fashion (with predetermined prayers); some people pray to God in a conversational way; some converse with God through their actions toward others; and still others communicate with God or the universe through their basic belief structure. How do you pray? How do you talk with God? How do you interact with the universe? Do you pray with reverence? Or are your prayers full of fear, cynicism, and anger? Your prayers reflect your inner life.

Ask yourself, "What do I need from my partner to help my spiritual life be as healthy as possible?" Communicate that need to your partner.

Focus Statement on Spiritual Health

I seek the face of God in everything I do and live my life in a way pleasing to the Creator.

Physical Health

What do you want your body to look like? What are your physical health goals? How long do you want to live? Your body is the vehicle that moves you through life. Your body's health is an integral part of your overall health. Your body has a linear relationship with your mind. When you feel good mentally, it helps your body feel well. When you are in great shape physically, it boosts your mental powers. So, just as you need emotional and intellectual goals to keep your mind on track, it is also essential to have clearly spelled out physical goals to keep your body in top shape.

What do you want for your body? Do you pollute your body with harmful habits? Or do you treat your body with the respect it deserves? Will your diet help you live longer? Or do you give it little real thought? How much do you want to weigh? Is your blood pressure in a healthy range? Are your muscles strong and toned, or are they flabby? These are essential questions to answer.

Here are fifteen tips I give my patients to feel healthy and live longer:

1. Be goal oriented with your health. Determine what you want for your body and health and go after it.

2. A healthy diet is essential. Did you know that every cell in your body makes itself new every five months? Literally, you are what you eat. The cells in your body consist of the nutrients (or lack thereof) you ingest. If you eat a lot of junk food, you will feel like junk. When you eat in a healthful way for several weeks you will feel a positive difference.

3. Water and water-rich foods are essential. Your body is 75-80 percent water. The body needs water to help flush the waste products out of its system, to cleanse itself. Without enough water your body

becomes dehydrated, and the toxins in your body negatively affect your cells. Water-rich foods are also a helpful source of water. Foods such as fruits (grapefruits, oranges, tomatoes, kiwis, etc.) and vegetables (lettuce, cabbage, squash, beans, etc.) are high in water content and great for the body.

4. Eat five to nine servings of fruits or vegetables a day. The National Cancer Institute, the National Academy of Sciences, and numerous universities and research centers have published studies that demonstrate a lower incidence of cancer for people who consume significant amounts of fruits and vegetables a day. One National Cancer Institute study was specific in its recommendations: eating at least five servings of fruits and vegetables a day will significantly lower your incidence of cancer; eating nine servings of fruits and vegetables a day will dramatically lower your risk of cancer. There is no question that a definite link exists between what you eat and cancer. Some people complain that it is hard to consume such high amounts of fruits and vegetables every day, but with forethought, it is not as hard as it might seem. For example:

- breakfast – a glass of juice (orange, apple, grapefruit, etc.) and a piece of fruit with cereal or toast; (two servings)
- snack – a piece of fruit (one serving)
- lunch – a mixed green salad, baked potato and a piece of fruit (three to four servings depending on the size and mixture of the salad)
- snack – chopped vegetables (carrots, celery, etc.) (one serving)
- dinner – a mixed green salad, hot vegetables, potato with a meat or pasta (three to four servings depending on the size and mixture of the salad and vegetables)
- Total = nine to eleven servings of fruits and vegetables a day

Cancer is the third leading cause of death in this

country. The proper diet lessens your chances of getting it.

5. Fiber-rich foods are also important. Dietary fiber is especially important for healthy intestinal systems and blood sugar levels. Fruits and vegetables are high in fiber, as are some breads and grain cereals. Fiber adds bulk your digestive system needs to process food. The bulk helps the food pass through your intestinal system quicker and easier, ridding your body of the toxins that are produced. Fiber-rich diets also have been shown to decrease blood sugar in diabetics. High blood sugar is toxic to your small blood vessels and can be a factor in heart and circulation problems.

6. Decrease the fat content in your diet. Fat-rich foods (meats, butter, whole milk, ice cream, oils, sauces, cakes, donuts, etc.) not only add weight to your system but also increase the fat in your body's bloodstream which places you at risk for heart problems or a stroke. People in my practice who have been the most successful at losing weight have changed their overall eating habits to include foods high in water content, high in fiber and fruits and vegetables, and low in fat. Fat is not sexy. You will appear more attractive to your partner with a healthy body.

7. Take a baby aspirin a day. Small doses of aspirin (a baby aspirin) have been shown to decrease the overall incidence of stroke and heart disease in adults. The anticoagulating properties prevent clots from forming and blocking off blood vessels which cause heart attacks or strokes. Make this part of your daily routine.

8. Exercise is essential to good health. In the fast pace of our society (long work hours, commuting, two-parent working families, etc.), exercise and personal care often are neglected. In addition, many technological advances of the past twenty years have reduced, or in some cases even eliminated, the need for physical activity and exertion in our daily lives. Such technological breakthroughs have led to inactive life-styles, and bodies that are losing their efficiency. Experts in nutrition, physiology, and medicine all agree

that a program of physical exertion on a continuing basis is required to maintain low body fat, a strong and healthy heart, and well-toned muscles. A well thought out exercise program will pay many dividends, including:

- more energy
- increased metabolism to help keep weight down
- improved circulation
- a lower incidence of heart disease and high blood pressure
- improved sleep
- decreased appetite
- increased muscle tone and a healthier looking body

Some form of daily exercise is best (walking, running, swimming, cycling, tennis), along with aerobic exercise (which increases your heart rate and causes your muscles to use oxygen to function) for at least twenty minutes three times a week. Many people hate exercise because they find it time consuming and boring. My advice is to keep trying different exercises until you find the one that suits you best.

I hate running. Swimming is too time consuming, and dries out my skin. A stationary bike didn't work any of my upper body muscles. I love tennis, but sometimes find it hard to find a partner or the time to play. My ski machine was the answer. After I worked out on it for a few weeks I found that it was easy to do, gave me an intense workout in a short period of time, and allowed me the convenience of showering at home and going on with my day. I like to turn up my *Phantom of the Opera* tape and exercise to the music. Stimulating music during exercise can help keep up your spirits and adrenalin.

Some sports do not require much exercise. For example, playing eighteen holes of golf (five hours) burns few calories and does not give you any aerobic exercise, even when you walk the course. I treated a man who was markedly overweight. He came to see me specifically to lose weight. I outlined my recommended strategies of nutrition and exercise. Several weeks after he started the program, he complained he wasn't losing any weight. When I asked about his exercise, he told me he was now playing two rounds of golf a week. When I told him that he needed continuous exercise for twenty minutes and that walking a golf course wasn't enough, because you walk for a while (100-200 yards) and then stop, hit the ball and then walk and stop and hit the ball again. He looked surprised and said, "Wait a minute doc, it's not quite like that. I get in the cart, go to the ball, hit it and then get back in the cart and go to the ball and hit it again. Think of all the exercise I'm doing getting in and out of the cart!" Don't fool yourself into believing that a little exercise is a lot.

9. Keep within ten pounds of your ideal body weight. Ideal body weight for women is often figured by allowing one hundred pounds for a five-foot woman and then adding six pounds per inch thereafter. For example, if a woman is five feet three inches, her ideal body weight would be:

5 feet	= 100 lbs.
3 inches (at 6 lbs./inch)	= 18 lbs.
total 5 feet 3 inches	= 118 lbs. ideal weight

(Add ten pounds to your ideal weight for a heavy boned frame, subtract ten pounds for a slim frame.)

Ideal body weight for a man is figured in a similar way: one hundred pounds for five feet, and six to seven pounds per inch thereafter. So a man who is five feet ten inches tall ideally should weigh 160-170 pounds. Again, this will vary depending on type of body frame.

People who are overweight have less energy, more health problems, are often discriminated against at work, and may be less attractive to their partners. Follow the suggestions in 1–8 for proper nutrition and exercise, and your weight will improve.

10. Slow, deep, belly breathing is healing. I teach almost all of my patients about the importance of breathing. Oxygen is essential to every single cell in your body, and correct breathing techniques increase the amount of oxygen in your body. Faulty breathing patterns cause problems with anxiety and poor concentration. Several times a day, stop and take ten deep breaths, expanding your belly as you breathe in. Also, do this whenever you are anxious, angry, or irritable. When most people become anxious they begin to hyperventilate (breathe faster), which makes their lungs inefficient and lowers the oxygen content in their bloodstreams. Counteracting this process with slow, deep breaths will give your body, and especially your brain, enough oxygen to calm down and feel good.

11. Shield yourself from the sun. The sun, besides increasing the risk of skin cancer, also causes dehydration, which drains energy as well as water.

12. Quit smoking. Live longer. Feel better. Help those around you to live longer.

13. Drink no more than three cups of coffee per day. Also watch other sources of caffeine, such as tea, sodas, chocolate. Caffeine provides a short-term energy boost, but it also causes rebound fatigue. Increase your energy with nutrition and exercise, not caffeine.

14. Do not drink more than two alcoholic beverages a day—two regular mixed drinks or one double; two six-ounce glasses of wine; or two six-ounce servings of beer. (Contrary to what many people believe, beer and wine are just as dangerous to your health as other forms of alcohol, and as potentially addictive.)

15. Maximize your energy cycle. If at all possible, do what is most important to you when you are the most effective.

Often, incorporating these health tips into your relationship can enhance follow through and effectiveness. Helping your partner care for his or her body pays you dividends in the long run. Keep your physical health actions consistent with your goals.

Ask yourself, "What do I need from my partner to

help my physical life be as healthy as possible."
Communicate that need to your partner.

FOCUS STATEMENT ON PHYSICAL HEALTH

My physical body is the vehicle that takes me
through life. Therefore, I provide my body with the
best care, nutrition, and exercise to keep myself alive,
toned, and healthy.

From a personal perspective, it is critical that you
believe that you are responsible for you. Too many
people blame their spouse, their lover, their business
partner, their children for their personal problems. They
say things such as:

- "I can't quit smoking because my job is too
  stressful."
- "I'll start losing weight after we go to marriage
  counseling."
- "I wish we went to church, but my husband
  won't go with me."
- "My kids won't eat vegetables, so I have no choice
  but to fix the foods they want."
- "I don't have any time to learn new things, I
  have too many responsibilities at home."

Take responsibility to make changes in your life and
this attitude will empower you for the rest of your life.

PERSONAL FOCUS STATEMENT

Meaning and Purpose: I am growing as an
individual and making a difference in the lives of others
whenever I can.

Intellectual Stimulation: I actively seek to stimulate
my brain by learning new information. I also seek a
give-and-take with others for the mutual benefit of
gaining and giving information, allowing the possibility
in my life of new ideas.

Emotional Health: I encourage myself to be
responsible, positive, focused, thoughtful, and to learn

from my mistakes. I am a good parent to myself, praising successful attitudes in myself and constructively correcting attitudes that hold me back.

Spiritual Health: I seek the face of God in everything I do and live my life in a way pleasing to the Creator.

Physical Health: My physical body is the vehicle that takes me through life. Therefore, I provide my body with the best care, nutrition, and exercise to keep myself alive, toned, and healthy.

Chapter 14

Constructing Your Two-Minute Focus Statement

What kind of relationship do you want with your partner? Is your behavior together getting you what you want? *Would You Give Two-Minutes a Day for a Lifetime of Love?* is about *total focus*. It offers you the direction and guidance your relationship needs to be fresh, satisfying, and fulfilling. It will help you take your attitudes and actions in the relationship out of your unconscious and place them squarely in the light of your wants and desires.

By now you have developed the individual pieces of the Two-Minute Focus Statement. This chapter is about putting it together. Everything gets filtered through your Two-Minute Focus Statement, every thought, every attitude, every action, and every plan. To make this program work for you, it is essential for you to become so familiar with your Two-Minute Focus Statement that you can immediately share it with your partner, your family, and your friends.

Directions: Both people in the relationship take out separate pieces of paper (or get into your word processor) and clearly write or type out your major goals and desires for your relationship. Do this separately the first time. Title the top of the page with "The Two-Minute Focus Statement." Then label the following main headings and subheadings:

THE TWO-MINUTE FOCUS STATEMENT

SHARED RELATIONAL FOCUS STATEMENT
Attitude and Assumptions:
Time:
Communication:
Child-Rearing:
Problem-Solving:

SHARED PHYSICAL LOVE FOCUS STATEMENT

SHARED FUN FOCUS STATEMENT

SHARED WORK FOCUS STATEMENT

SHARED MONEY FOCUS STATEMENT

SHARED PERSONAL FOCUS STATEMENT
Meaning and Purpose:
Intellectual Stimulation:
Emotional Health:
Spiritual Health:
Physical Health:

Next to each subheading, succinctly write out what is important to you in that area; write what you want, not what you don't want. Be positive and use first person. Also, write what you want with confidence and the expectation you will make it happen. Keep the paper with you so that you can work on it over several days.

After both of you finish your individual drafts of the Two-Minute Focus Statement, together write out a master statement that combines your goals, wants, and desires. First, look for areas of agreement, don't get bogged down in the little things (review the chapter on negotiation). Next, list the areas you are having problems with and go through the problem-solving steps in the chapter on shared relational focus. Here is the combined draft of the Two-Minute Focus Statement my wife and I wrote.

THE TWO-MINUTE FOCUS STATEMENT

SHARED RELATIONAL FOCUS STATEMENT:

Attitude and Assumptions: to have positive basic assumptions toward each other in an encouraging, supportive, and positive atmosphere.

Time: we spend daily special time together; some of the best time of our week is spent together; we compromise and alternate choosing how we spend our time together.

Communication: we have two-way communication that is active, persistent, clear and positive.

Child-Rearing: as parents we are involved, open, firm, together, kind, and fun; for our children we act in a way to help them be relational, responsible, independent, self-confident, self-accepting, adaptable, emotionally free, and fun.

Problem-Solving: We are able to solve problems in an attitude of care and respect by taking time to define the problem, clearly state our differing positions, understand the issues from the other person's point of view, list our options, make a decision, and then monitor the outcome.

SHARED PHYSICAL LOVE FOCUS STATEMENT

We actively seek excitement, passion, and sensuality in an atmosphere of fun and mutual giving. We will include lots of nonsexual and sexual touching to promote connectedness and bonding.

SHARED FUN FOCUS STATEMENT

Fun, freshness, and laughter are priorities in our relationship. We realize that these things are essential to health and make life's problems a lot easier to handle together. We actively look for ways to contribute lightheartedness and good fun to the relationship.

SHARED WORK FOCUS STATEMENT

In our work, both in and out of the home, we seek to share the tasks in a fair and equal way that allows both of us some of the sweat and some of the glory. We seek to help each other whenever possible and make the work we do meaningful, useful, and in line with the major goals we have for our life together.

SHARED MONEY FOCUS STATEMENT

Money and finances are issues we share and talk about. We choose to both be "in the know" about our money. Sound money management is essential to the overall health of our relationship. We share with each other thoughts on the best ways to obtain and save money. We spend our resources in a way consistent with our short-term and long-term goals. We balance frugality with the ability to spend our resources on fun and pleasure.

SHARED PERSONAL FOCUS STATEMENT

We seek to help each other reach our individual goals, knowing that will strengthen our bond together.

Meaning and Purpose: I am growing as an individual and making a difference in the lives of others whenever I can.

Intellectual Stimulation: I actively seek to stimulate my brain by learning new information. I also seek a give-and-take with others for the mutual benefit of gaining and giving information, allowing the possibility in my life of new ideas.

Emotional Health: I encourage myself to be responsible, positive, focused, thoughtful, and to learn from my mistakes. I am a good parent to myself, praising successful attitudes in myself and constructively correcting attitudes that hold me back.

Spiritual Health: I seek the face of God in everything I do and live my life in a way pleasing to the Creator.

Physical Health: My physical body is the vehicle that takes me through life. To that end, I provide my body with the best care, nutrition, and exercise to keep myself alive, toned and vibrant.

After you finish the combined draft, place this piece of paper where you, as a couple, can see it every day, such as on your refrigerator, by your bedside, or on the bathroom mirror. In that way, every day you can focus your eyes on what's important to you in your relationship. As you read through the statement, hear yourself saying the words with meaning and conviction. Seeing the words helps program your mind to act in a way consistent with your goals. This makes it easier to match your behavior to what you want. Your relationship becomes more conscious and you spend your time and energy on goals that are important to the relationship.

Once a month, set up a review session for you and your partner to go over and update your Two-Minute Focus Statement. First, notice what you like and provide positive feedback in the areas where you are doing well together. Talk about the problem areas in an atmosphere of care and concern. Use the problem-solving methods to work through difficulties. Whenever needed, revise your Two-Minute Focus Statement. Keep it updated, fresh, and a part of your daily routine for the rest of your life.

How is it going to be at the end of your life? Will you have worked for the goals in your relationship that were important to you? Or will you have worked for other people's goals and ignored yourself and your relationship? It is up to you. Use The Two-Minute Focus Statement to help your relationship be the best ever.

———————◆———————

Dr. Amen welcomes your stories and/or comments on how this program has helped you. You may contact him at:

2220 Boynton Street, Suite C
Fairfield, CA 94533
(707) 429-7181 Fax: (707) 429-8210